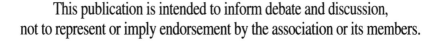

This publication is intended to inform debate and discussion,
not to represent or imply endorsement by the association or its members.

# Presidential Search

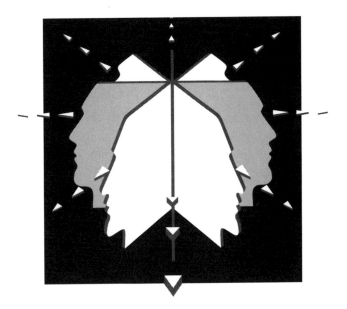

A Guide to the Process
of Selecting and Appointing
College and University Presidents

Charles B. Neff ▪ Barbara Leondar
A Revision of the Original Work by John W. Nason

Association of Governing Boards of Universities and Colleges

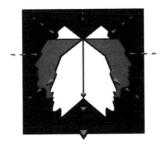

# CONTENTS

## CHAPTER FOUR:

## CHAPTER FIVE:

## CHAPTER SIX:

AGB gratefully acknowledges the generous

contributions of the AT&T Foundation and the

Teachers Insurance and Annuity Association—

College Retirement Equities Fund, which made

this book possible.

# ACKNOWLEDGMENTS

The authors gratefully acknowledge several individuals who contributed to the positive elements of this volume. The defects are attributable to the authors alone.

John W. Nason, who wrote the original *Presidential Search* in 1980 and its first revision in 1984, is widely known, by virtue of his judgment and wisdom, as the dean of those who have advised us on presidential searches in colleges and universities. His pioneering efforts to bring practical advice into an increasingly complex and occasionally ineffective process have been instrumental in educating us all. His work has greatly influenced this new version of *Presidential Search*.

AGB Vice President for Publications Dan Levin and Senior Editor Donna Fowler have been, as usual, wonderful colleagues and editors. AGB President Bob Gale and Executive Vice President Tom Ingram provided extensive and valuable comments on an early draft.

With patience, humor, and competence, Lynn Biggs and Alisa Riggs have been our clerical mainstays—and more.

We would not have done it without all their help.

Barbara Leondar
Charles B. Neff
September 1992

# Foreword

    AGB is deeply indebted to John W. Nason, author of the original *Presidential Search*, for his exemplary work on this important topic. Nason, who served as president of Swarthmore and Carleton colleges, is one of America's most respected educators and experts on academic trusteeship. In 1973-74, he directed a seminal study of lay trusteeship in the United States, one of his many contributions to American higher education and one that laid the foundation for the development of a body of knowledge on the concept and practice of citizen trusteeship.

    From his unique vantage point as an academic president, trustee, and student of trusteeship, Nason gleaned a host of wise insights that he has generously shared with the higher education community over his long and distinguished career. Because the selection of a president is the most important task a board of trustees undertakes, he also shrewdly saw that the way a presidential search is planned, conducted, and concluded is nearly as important as the outcome itself. Nason drew upon his own wealth of experience and the counsel of an outstanding national advisory board to produce the original *Presidential Search* for AGB in 1980. That volume was revised for the first time in 1984, and in 1992 Charles B. Neff and Barbara Leondar drew upon their multifaceted experience as search consultants to expand upon Nason's earlier work, fashioning a comprehensive approach to presidential search. This volume has proved so popular it now is in its second printing.

    Adhering to Nason's dictum that no single, perfect method exists for every institution and that each institution must tailor the search process to its own needs and circumstances, Neff and Leondar offer useful options and guidelines that will help institutions conduct a successful search. They have assembled a clear, compelling, and up-to-date description of the opportunities, considerations, cautions, and detailed plans that comprise a good search process.

    In late 1996, the Commission on the Academic Presidency issued its report, *Renewing the Academic Presidency: Stronger Leadership for Tougher Times.* Sponsored by AGB, this independent national commission of 21 distinguished citizens–including eight former college and university presidents–called attention to the need to think differently and smarter about how academic institutions should be governed, managed, and led. Its report also is worth reading by search committees. Among its recommendations for governing boards are these:

- *Select presidents who are truly capable of leading as change agents and risk takers.* While many candidates will be found on campuses, a reservoir of talent remains to be tapped in the worlds of business, government, the professions, the nonprofit sector, and the military. Trustees should not shy away from potential presidents from nontraditional backgrounds.
- *Provide presidents with the contractual support they require.* College and university boards should establish a compensation system for presidents that recognizes the risks of leadership.

AGB is planning a major study of the many complex issues concerning chief executive compensation and conditions of employment, as recommended by the commission. And a new book on presidential (and board) assessment, written by Pat McPherson, president emerita of Bryn Mawr College; Barry Munitz, chancellor of the California State University System; and William A. Weary, former AGB staff member and presidential search consultant, will be published in 1998. In the interim, the association has various resources on these subjects.

We wish you and your institution a successful search experience, with every confidence that this book will help to make it so.

Richard T. Ingram
AGB President
June 1997

# INTRODUCTION

Colleges and universities are mutable institutions; they go through development cycles. Sometimes they are in a growth phase; sometimes they must consolidate. Sometimes they will concentrate on curricular change, while at other times they may react to changing enrollment demographics or focus on a major capital campaign. A college or university president must attend to a complex array of responsibilities and duties, many of which remain the same regardless of the phase of development of the institution. Yet in each of these cycles a different type of leader may be required.

The search for a college or university president is, above all, an attempt to find a leader whose skills, interests, and background match the needs of an institution in a particular phase of its development. Even within the same institution, no two presidential searches will be exactly the same. A clear statement of the leadership qualities an institution seeks must be created separately for each search.

In many ways, a presidential search is the most important task a governing board undertakes. For it is through the person of the chief executive officer that board policy will be successfully—or unsuccessfully—implemented and through whom many of the creative impulses for institutional development will be brought before the board.

Boards should see leadership change as part of larger cycles of institutional change and development. A board, understandably, wants to stay with a president as long as possible. Nevertheless, thinking constructively about the next phase of institutional development, even in the midst of a successful presidential tenure, may be in the college's or university's best long-term interest. The links between day-to-day operations, planning, and leadership continually needs to be examined, partly for the short-term operations of the institution but also for its long-term health. It is not desirable for a board to begin to think about where it is going and what kind of leader it needs when—and only when—it faces a leadership change.

If policies, programs, mission, and resources are not well synchronized, the institution will face a leadership crisis. From this perspective, institutional planning, presidential service, evaluation of presidential leadership, and presidential search can be seen as parts of a larger process. If they are viewed in these terms, a smooth transition from one chief executive to another is most likely.

CHAPTER ONE

# Reviewing the Process of Search and Selection

When a vacancy occurs in the presidency of a college or university, the board of trustees must decide a series of preliminary issues before the work of the search can actually begin. It must determine how the search and selection committees will be structured, who will be invited to serve, what instructions will be issued, whether outside consultants will be employed, and whether a transitional CEO is needed. The following pages explore each of these issues in sequence. When the board begins its deliberations, however, it will quickly discover that these fundamental decisions cannot easily be sorted into a series of pigeonholes. Every issue impinges on each of the others, and thus decisions made in early discussions may need to be modified in later ones.

Because these interlocking decisions will lay the foundation for the entire presidential search, it is important to give them the weight and attention they deserve. Time invested in formulating these early decisions will pay off later when the search begins in earnest.

## Search, Screen, Select

In establishing a search procedure, no act of the board is more significant than the instructions it issues to all concerned about the roles they will play and the boundaries among those roles. Basically, the board must help the campus constituencies and those surrounding the university to understand the differences among three principal functions: *searching*, *screening*, and *selecting*.

It is solely the responsibility of the board to *select* the chief executive officer of an institution, and the board must structure all policies so this is made abundantly clear and procedurally possible. The board should be absolutely certain at the beginning of the process how it wants to handle the end of the process. How many candidates does it wish to have recommended by a screening committee (if one is established)? In what form will the candidates be recommended to the board (ranked, unranked, with or without recommendations)? Where and how will the board meet one or more of the finalist candidates?

Above all, the board should ensure that the screening committee will not usurp the function of the board by selecting one finalist candidate whom the board can only accept or reject. The board may wish to give its representatives on the search committee considerable authority in pointing the board toward the selection of a particular individual. But the ultimate selection must rest with the board itself.

By contrast, *screening* is ordinarily accomplished by a committee designated by the board. Unless prohibited by sunshine laws, a screening committee normally operates in confidence. Using criteria established by the board, its principal purpose is to evaluate a large number of preliminary candidates and to reduce them to finalist candidates who are forwarded to the board. Screening is the principal and exclusive function of a screening committee, a function shared not even by the board itself and, certainly, not by other constituencies in the academic community.

*Searching*, properly conducted, is an activity in which all members of the academic community and friends of the campus can be invited to participate. The importance of a vigorous search should not be underestimated. Talented candidates need to be sought out and actively recruited. The greater the number of institutional supporters who can be enlisted in this effort, and the wider the net they cast, the more effective the search will be. Once the criteria for leadership are published, students, faculty, alumni, friends, board members, and even interested citizens can be invited to submit nominations. An institution is strengthened by receiving a large number of qualified nominations and also by involving many people, giving them a sense of significant participation in the search process.

# Setting Up the Search Process

The board of trustees may create or activate one or more committees to carry out the work of the search. In the case of public institutions and increasingly among independent institutions as well, bylaws sometimes specify the composition of the committee(s) and the procedures to be followed. If procedures already exist, they should be thoroughly reviewed before being implemented. In each situation, however, individuals must be chosen to serve and the machinery set in motion. Unless the machinery of search and selection already has been determined, the board has four options.

- It can constitute itself a committee of the whole or create a special board committee to carry out the entire search.
- It can appoint a single search and screening committee with representatives from various constituencies.
- It can establish two committees, one to search and one to screen.
- Finally, it can appoint a trustee committee plus one or more advisory committees of faculty, students, and others.

When a board is relatively small, its members may prefer to keep control of the entire process in their own hands. In those church-related colleges or universities where it is stipulated that the president must be a member of the religious order or denomination, the number of available candidates often is so small and the individuals so well known that the board can proceed without setting up committees of search and selection. Occasionally, an internal candidate is so obvious a choice that the board makes the appointment, preferably in consultation with the faculty, without undertaking a search. But these are special situations. In most instances the exclusion of faculty and other constituencies eventually will prove counterproductive. If such constituencies are not in some way included, they may exercise their dissatisfaction in challenging the legitimacy of the next president instead of concentrating on constructive collaboration.

Most commonly, governing boards establish a single search and screening committee. Normally, such a committee is composed of trustees and faculty; frequently, alumni, administrative officers, line staff, and representatives of the community also are asked to serve. Students may or not be included, depending on the traditions of the institution in this regard, as well as its mission and scope.

Such a committee can benefit from the diverse perspectives and the unique insights of its members. Its discussions can have a beneficial unifying effect. Typical is the statement by the search committee chair of a state university: "Our process worked so well that the individual constituencies became a committee of the whole and disregarded their particular loyalties. As a result, nothing would deter them from seeking the most highly qualified candidate for the presidency." Properly instructed and constituted, a committee will transform itself through its work from a collection of special interests into an informed and effective instrument of the academic institution.

A less common method is the establishment of two committees—one for search and screening and the second for selection of the final acceptable candidates. The former usually consists of faculty, students, and others, with one or two trustees as liaison (though some have no trustees), while the latter is composed of trustees only (frequently the executive committee). This arrangement has the advantage of dividing up the work and, in particular, of assigning the most time-consuming stages, the search and preliminary screening, to a representative group. It reassures constituencies—faculty in particular, but also, where appropriate, alumni, sponsoring groups, or local citizens—that the new president will be acceptable to them, because those not acceptable will have been screened out.

A problem is likely to develop if the committees charged with searching and screening are not given clear instructions about how candidates are to be evaluated and forwarded to the board. A committee may usurp the selection function, which is the board's exclusive responsibility. It can dictate the final choice by concluding that only one candidate is suitable or by giving one individual so strong a priority rating as to amount to the same thing. The board chair of a distinguished private university, for example, reports: "The search was originated on the theory that there would be a search committee to screen candidates and recommend five to six qualified candidates to the selection committee.... However, the search committee, and particularly the faculty and students thereof, began to regard themselves as the selection committee."

This leads to the fourth option—a search and screening committee composed of trustees, buttressed by a series of advisory committees representing faculty, students, alumni, and occasionally others. This arrangement permits consultation with various constituencies, while still keeping the selection process in the hands of those primarily responsible for the final appointment. It helps to avoid the polarization between trustees and these other groups that can occur when strong differences of opinion are expressed. On the other hand, communication problems can create irritation, and faculty and students often resent what they consider second-class participation in the search process. Confusion about role, scope, and influence also are likely.

Within these four options, the choice of committee structure will vary with the institution and should be made with individual circumstances in mind. Here and elsewhere, flexibility should be a guiding principle. The temper of the campus and the degree of trust among trustees, administration, faculty, and students will influence the choice. Where relations are strained, the committee structure is especially important and should be given careful thought. Where relations are reasonably harmonious, structure may seem less important, but still should be clearly specified.

The single committee composed of representatives of several constituencies is the most common structure. It avoids the difficulties of communication and logistics that often plague multiple committees. Its outstanding advantage is the strong sense of unity and common enterprise that the joint work of the committee generates. The most common evaluation of individuals who have worked on such committees is that they produce new perspectives and broader understanding among trustees, faculty, and students working together for a common goal. Unless compelling reasons exist to organize the process differently, the single committee is best. It seems consistently to produce the most positive results—in process, in communication, and in eventual selection.

# Size of the Search Committee

The size of search or advisory committees will vary according to the pattern outlined in the previous section. Single committees tend to be larger and multiple committees, smaller. A small committee may be easier to assemble and can work efficiently. On the other hand, the value of a committee representing various constituencies must not be minimized. The trade-off between size and representation will have to be made, but experience suggests that a committee of nine to fifteen works best. Larger committees need not be less effective, but large groups take longer to organize, meetings last longer, and maintaining confidentiality can be a problem.

# Composition of the Committee

Just as some trustees look upon faculty as "employees" with no proper voice in policy decisions or presidential appointments, some faculty view trustees as nonacademics who know nothing about education and should not be involved in so important an exercise as selecting a president. Fortunately, such individuals usually are in the minority. Most boards recognize the legitimate concern of faculty in the selection process and vice versa.

"Joint effort" is specifically recommended in the formal *Statement on Government of Colleges and Universities*, issued in 1966 by the American Association of University Professors and recognized by AGB as a significant step forward in the clarification of the respective roles of governing boards, faculties, and administrations. It states in part: "The selection of a chief administrative officer should follow upon cooperative search by the governing board and the faculty, taking into consideration the opinions of others who are appropriately interested. The president should be equally qualified to serve both as the executive officer of the governing board and as the chief academic officer of the institution and the faculty. The president's dual role requires an ability to interpret to board and faculty the educational views and concepts of institutional government of the other. The president should have the confidence of the board and the faculty."

Each board ultimately is responsible for the search process and, in the end, decides who shall serve. Faculty, student, and other participation is by invitation and privilege, not by right. A board may be unwise not to include faculty and others, but it has no legal obligation to do so unless bylaws or state regulations dictate membership. The guiding principle should be to approach this issue with the objective of giving the person ultimately selected the greatest possible amount of credibility and acceptance by all constituent groups.

# Selecting Committee Members

A good committee will be one with a high degree of mutual respect and trust among its members. This may not exist at first, but with the right selection of members and with the leadership of the chair, it should emerge as the result of working toward a shared objective.

What qualities should one seek in committee members? Among them are demonstrable commitment to the institution, an understanding of its programs and problems, breadth of experience, a capacity for balanced judgment and discretion, and the ability to recognize and respect the validity and integrity of differing viewpoints. Ideally, the committee should reflect the diversity of the institution by including women and members of minority groups.

This is a large order, of course. How does one arrive at a committee composed of such people?

In some instances, the board may choose to have its executive committee or its chair make all appointments. Presumably, other members of the community will make suggestions regarding the nontrustee members. This method has the advantage of making reasonably sure that difficult or potentially disruptive members will not serve, although it is likely to anger faculty and students by denying them a voice in the process.

The most common (and probably ideal) practice is for each constituent group to select its own member(s) to serve. Sometimes the board or faculty will seek to control the selection of students, but in general, faculty choose faculty members, and students pick student members. The alumni association may ask one or more of the officers of the association (already elected by the alumni) to serve ex officio. This gives the various constituencies the greatest sense of participation; and, if there is full agreement on the person chosen, the new president starts his or her career with a high degree of acceptance. While there is no certainty that the committee will be widely perceived as representative of diverse interests within the institution or that the resulting mixture will be harmonious and cooperative, conscientious effort to provide communication through effective representation is important.

One way of reducing the disadvantages of allowing each group to designate its own members is to have the board establish general criteria for selecting committee members. It may specify, for example, that one faculty member should be chosen by each division of the university, that there should be an equal number of senior and junior members of the faculty, that one student should come from a graduate or professional school and the other from the undergraduate college, or that one student should be male and the other female.

A second way is to invite various constituencies to nominate several candidates for committee membership with the understanding that the board or the chair will appoint committee members from among those nominated. This allows the board a certain latitude in ensuring fair representation and diversity on the committee, while recognizing the legitimate wish of faculty, students, and others to have a real voice in the matter.

It is not uncommon for the board chair to serve on the committee. No trustee works more closely with the president, and the board chair's presence on the committee ensures the selection of finalists with whom a positive rapport can be built.

Not everyone agrees, however, that the board chair should serve on the committee. Often, the chair is a strong and powerful personality and may dominate the committee. Occasionally, the chair pushes for a favorite candidate over the opposition of the committee, usually with unfortunate results. The board chair also might consider that his or her principal function is to guide the final selection, a function that could be diluted or compromised through participation in the screening process. An observer status for the board chair is always a possibility, provided everyone understands that the screening committee deliberations should not be reported to noncommittee board members.

A less controversial point is the role of the affirmative-action officer. Regardless of whether the affirmative-action officer is invited to serve on the committee, he or she certainly should be consulted to make sure that policies and procedures are appropriate.

There are obvious advantages in having a seasoned and trusted administrative officer on the committee. He or she will know better than most the nature of the president's job and will be able to assess candidates in the light of that knowledge. On the other hand, such an officer may be too close to the president's office for comfort; his or her opinions may carry more weight than they deserve. Clearly, no administrator who might conceivably be a candidate or who has been personally too identified with the outgoing president should serve on a screening committee. In addition, it is questionable whether an officer who will report directly to the new president should participate in his or her selection.

# The Charge to the Committee

Concurrent with or prior to decisions about what kind of committee to establish, the board should draft a clear written statement of the committee's mandate. The board should make sure everyone interested in the selection of the new president—the campus community, the alumni, and even the press—knows the composition of the committee and the extent of its authority. A board may elect to leave procedural details largely to the committee, but without a clear general charge, the committee will later run into difficulty if the extent and limits of its responsibility are not made clear at the outset. Items that might be included in the charge are the following:

1. Development of a statement of leadership qualities sought in the new president (unless the board already has developed such a statement).

2. Membership of the committee(s), including either the name of the chair (if from the board) or suggestions on how to choose the chair.

3. The date by which the board expects recommendations of nominees from the committee.

4. The breadth of search for candidates. Some boards have instructed their committees on where to look; others leave this to the committees themselves.

5. The necessity of complying with board policies (and, where relevant, system policies) as well as state and federal law, including equal opportunity/affirmative action and right-to-know legislation.

6. The availability of funds for committee expenses.

7. The option of using outside experienced executive-search consultants.

8. The degree of confidentiality or openness (e.g., sunshine laws) expected of the committee.

9. The number of candidates to be recommended to the board for final decision, whether these candidates are to be ranked, and whether names only or names accompanied by supporting statements should be forwarded.

10. The board's intention to make the final choice and set terms of appointment.

All of the foregoing do not necessarily need to be included in a formal charge to the committee, but most should be. (A sample committee charge is included in the appendix as Exhibit A.) To clear the air regarding the committee's responsibilities and authority, it helps to make the committee's mandate public.

# Use of Consultants

Early in the process, the board must decide whether to employ outside professional help or to offer the search committee this option. Outside assistance can range from using one or more consultants—usually former administrators or faculty members whose specialty is educational administration—to relying on a consulting firm. Some of the major commercial firms, which have made their reputations identifying top officers for business enterprises, now include similar services for nonprofit organizations. Recent years have seen the birth of a new family of consulting firms designed to provide a variety of services to educational institutions, among them specialists in the recruitment of top academic officers.

The decision to use outside help is sometimes delegated to the search committee. In that case, the board must provide the committee with discretionary funds for this purpose. Often the choice of a particular consultant is left to the committee, within cost guidelines laid down by the board.

Outside consultants and professional firms may be used for a variety of purposes: to advise and assist in setting up the committee's procedures, to help define the institution's needs and establish desirable criteria, to develop and screen a pool of candidates, to conduct interviews, to interview references and check candidates' credentials, and even to participate in the final evaluation and recommendation.

If the search for college and university presidents is becoming increasingly difficult and complex, why do more institutions not make use of competent professional help? Some people say doing so is not part of the academic tradition. Faculty, and to a lesser extent trustees, have an instinctive distrust of an outsider's ability to understand and appreciate academic values or the special quality of "our" institution. Sometimes they suspect consultants of wanting to manipulate the process in favor of a predetermined candidate. These myths and prejudices have been eroded by the entry of consultants who possess academic credentials as former faculty members, deans, or presidents.

Expense is another factor. Major business-oriented management companies charge 30 percent to 33 percent of the first year's salary and benefits of the appointee; nonprofit consulting firms ordinarily quote a flat fee, depending on the amount of work involved.

Consulting fees represent a significant part of the total cost of a search, but they can be a good investment. Compared with the cost of hiring the wrong person, consulting fees are negligible. After all, the new president's impact will be felt not only during the period of service but will also reverberate throughout the institution's history. Viewed from this perspective, parsimony appears short-sighted. Generous funding of a well-conducted search, including funds for the purchase of outside expertise, is not an extravagance; it is the cost of insuring the institution's future health.

In many cases, trustees and faculty members believe they have sufficient competence to run their own show. In most statewide systems, one or more central office administrators assist member colleges or universities in choosing new presidents; often, they maintain a current roster of potential candidates. Their involvement in frequent searches often obviates the need for outside help. Some private colleges will have on their boards one or more trustees who previously have been through the process and who are prepared to play an active role a second time. But this is the exception rather than the rule.

David Riesman and Judith B. McLaughlin argue that increasingly talented presidential candidates will need to be sought out and wooed.[1] Many people will aspire to the position, but really top-notch candidates may not apply. Such individuals already have good positions and will be most offended (and possibly damaged) by premature publicity. Consultants can be especially helpful in identifying and negotiating with these people.

There are, of course, other reasons for seeking professional assistance. An outside consultant can be of great value in a crisis situation where an institution has had two or more presidents in rapid succession, where the departure of the previous president was stormy, or where feelings of distrust and antagonism affect the attitudes of faculty, students, and trustees. For inexperienced committees that might be a little fearful of proceeding alone, the experienced consultant can provide direction and support. For example, when a consultant conducts the delicate and diplomatic background checks on the finalists before the committee makes its recommendation, the work generally is more skillful (and is less apt to cause premature disclosure). Most important, when an institution needs a particular combination of abilities and experience to move forward, a consultant's skill in locating such individuals can be invaluable.

Institutions can choose from a considerable variety of commercial consulting firms. There are many fewer nonprofit search agencies, and only one is part of a tax-exempt higher education association—the Presidential Search Consultation Service (PSCS) of the Association of Governing Boards of Universities and Colleges.

# Choosing an Acting or Interim President

When presidents retire or otherwise announce their resignation well in advance, there is time for the machinery of search and selection to function in a satisfactory fashion. When, however, the president dies, becomes too ill to serve, accepts another job, or leaves under pressure and on short notice, the board faces an emergency. Should it engage in a crash program to find a new president, or should it appoint an acting or interim president?

In an article on the transitional presidency, Charles B. Neff suggests that an *acting president* is one who serves for a brief but indefinite period of time, exercising some of the powers of the presidency though probably not the full range associated with that office.[2] An *interim president* holds the position of president for a specified period and assumes a more specific list of duties to be accomplished. An acting president can often be a candidate for the permanent presidency; an interim president should not be a candidate.

Neff also lists ten considerations for a board to examine before determining whether the institution would benefit from an acting or interim president:

1. Does an emergency situation exist, requiring someone immediately to assume the presidency?

2. How does the board wish a transitional presidency to be related to the process of seeking permanent leadership?

3. What specifically does the board want the acting or interim president to accomplish?

4. How long should the temporary president serve?

5. Does the campus have a natural insider for the transitional president's job?

6. Who is a proper outsider, and how can the board find such a person?

7. If an outsider, does an interim president need to possess all the qualities the board seeks in the permanent president?

8. How can the temporary president help the board in the transition to the permanent presidency?

9. In what way will the transitional president be announced to the campus community?

10. Is the board satisfied that it was prepared for the eventuality of a temporary presidency?

Usually, an acting or interim president is sought in response to an emergency. Less frequently, a board may wish to consider an interim president for the purpose of addressing major institutional issues that need correction. Reorganization, making personnel changes, closing a branch, or changing a major academic program would be examples.

In either case, the selection of an acting or interim chief executive will affect the full search in a variety of ways. When naming an appointee, the board will want to specify unambiguously this individual's relation to the search that will eventually begin, and the board should relate the task of the interim president to the kind of president sought for the next stage of the institution's development.

# Moving Ahead

The foregoing issues cannot be resolved by formula. When discussing how to proceed with a presidential search, each board must consider the particulars of its own campus. Size, age, mission, and history inevitably will color each decision. But when a board has explored and finally resolved these issues to its own satisfaction, it will have prepared the foundations for a productive search. Now the work can proceed.

---

[1] David Riesman and Judith B. McLaughlin, "Executive Recruiters in Search for College Presidents," unpublished paper, 1983. See also the more extensive discussion in "The Use of Consultants," Judith Block McLaughlin and David Riesman, *Choosing a College President* (Princeton, N.J.: The Carnegie Foundation for the Advancement of Teaching 1990), pp. 225–262.

[2] Charles B. Neff, "The Transitional Presidency," *AGB Reports*, September/October 1989 (vol. 31, no. 5) pp. 16–21.

## CHAPTER TWO

# Formulating the Criteria

The objective of the presidential selection process is to match a person and an institution. Cycles of institutional development and leadership abilities can thus be aligned.

## The Board's Responsibility

Underlying a presidential search are these propositions: (1) the selection of the new president is the major responsibility of the board of trustees; (2) the board must, therefore, determine the criteria and process by which the new president will be chosen; and (3) these criteria should be derived from a thorough analysis of institutional objectives and needs over the institution's next period of development.

Some boards, especially among community colleges, will themselves undertake the institutional analysis and/or formulate the qualities the new president should possess. Other boards, faced with a change in administration, will turn to the academic community for an evaluation of institutional goals and problems, from which a list of presidential characteristics can be derived. These suggestions then can be modified or endorsed by the board and given to the selection committee as a part of its official mandate. Boards occasionally find themselves in the fortunate situation of having recently completed long-range plans or the kind of institutional appraisal required for reaccreditation. Both are invaluable in preparation for a presidential search.

In a majority of cases, however, the formulation of criteria is part of the mandate to the search and screening committee. Occasionally, where more than one committee is part of the process, the advisory committees as well as the search and screening committee (which manages the process) are charged with this mandate. As a rule, committees then refer their conclusions to the board for official approval. Another useful technique, if time allows, is for a committee to publish its tentative criteria for the new president, hold public hearings or invite written responses, and then publish a final version that represents substantial agreement within the larger community. If the board asked for clearance in its original instructions to the screening committee, the final version should be sent to the board for approval before publication. In any case, the board should make clear where final approval for the statement rests.

# The Institutional Analysis

The practice of deriving presidential criteria from an appraisal of an institution's present condition and future prospects is conventional wisdom in theory and largely ignored in practice. Boards and search committees alike have a tendency to rush into the search and selection of candidates without taking adequate stock of what or whom they really need. An important lesson for committees to comprehend is the desirability of examining their institutions before deciding what kind of individual endowed with what kind of talents will cope most successfully over the coming decade.

Judith McLaughlin and David Riesman say it well: "If a successful search is to be conducted, the search committee must have a clear sense of the sort of person for whom they are searching. The starting point of the search process, then, should be introspection concerning what the institution needs in order to reorganize strengths and to cope with weaknesses, both in terms of history and tradition, and future prospects and dilemmas....Without an institutional assessment and leadership definition, the search committee is also at a loss to know who will be the best choice for them. They run the risk of choosing someone totally inappropriate for their institution, someone whose attractiveness lies in the fact that his or her style differs from the departing president, or someone whose understanding of the college or university is too limited for effective leadership."[1]

How should the trustees or the screening committee go about the business of taking institutional stock? There is rarely time for the elaborate type of self-study that boards might well authorize at less critical moments.[2] One needs to know something about the present condition of the college or university, about the problems looming on the horizon, and about the direction the institution must go to maintain its position, enhance its reputation, improve its services, or merely to stay alive. This is a stage at which competent and experienced consultants can be of great value. A checklist of issues relevant to public, private, two-year, four-year, and graduate institutions appears in the appendix as Exhibit B.

The institutional analysis may be conducted particularly for a presidential search, or it may have already been available through ongoing institutional planning efforts. Institutional analysis is an absolutely necessary but never sufficient ingredient in a successful presidential search. Institutional analysis can serve as the basis for developing a usable set of leadership criteria to describe the next president, but developing such criteria is a *discrete and critical exercise in its own right*.

# Development of Leadership Criteria

Many institutions develop valid and usable leadership criteria. But in many others the criteria are either unsatisfactory or unusable because they fail in one of three specific ways.

First, there is often confusion between a *job description* and a statement of *leadership criteria*. A job description specifies the official duties and responsibilities of the president. In the case of public institutions, that job description is often codified in administrative procedure or law. Clearly, it is necessary that a job description for a president exist, but such a description is almost always a universal and not very helpful compendium of the full range of duties and responsibilities of the office. It fails to include a description of the qualities an institution might seek in a particular leader for a particular stage of its development.

Second, *personal* qualities are often given precedence over *professional* accomplishment. Although a leader must exhibit both personal and professional strengths, it is helpful to separate rather than mix the two in a statement of leadership criteria. For instance, every president should have the physical and emotional stamina to work long hours under considerable stress, and such moral qualities as honesty, courage, and respect for others. But if these are general expectations, they can be stated in a preamble to a true statement of leadership qualities. Leadership qualities should focus on the professional experience and capabilities required to lead the institution in the next few years.

Finally, for all intents and purposes, a statement of leadership qualities can fail if it becomes only an exercise in describing an ideal leader. Even if a committee does not begin with this premise, it sometimes ends up with such a statement because it keeps adding to its list every conceivable good quality a leader might possess. The proverbial fourteen points of perfection are little more useful to a committee than no statement at all. Since the ideal person does not exist, no one will ever exemplify all the criteria. Furthermore, simply listing ideal qualities diverts a committee from wrestling with real institutional issues and needs.

What should be included in a statement of leadership qualities? First, a committee should attempt to be relatively selective. It should concentrate on perhaps four or five principal professional qualities that are the most essential in the new president. Achieving some agreement on these qualities within the committee and/or among the various constituencies of the college or university community is an important first step in its own right. A list that grows by accretion is less useful than a more compact list of carefully defined qualities.

One means for achieving sharpness of definition is to write a paragraph for each of the principal qualities identified. For instance, if the person is expected to be an academic leader, what will that mean in practice? Is the institution seeking an innovator, a consolidator? Someone who will emphasize general education or the development of a particular new program? Or someone who understands a collective-bargaining environment? There are many kinds of academic leaders, and a particular kind may be the one most necessary at this time in the institution's history.

The same kind of description can be developed for other qualities. If a campus seeks a good manager, what does that term really mean, and what type of style is expected from the new president? Or if a fund-raiser is sought, what is meant by *that* term? Dealing with the legislature? Seeking funds from foundations? Corporations? Individuals? Or a combination of all of these?

The more precise the statement of leadership qualities can be, the more likely it is to be useful in a variety of additional ways. A careful statement of leadership criteria can also be used as a recruiting device. It can and should serve as the basis for advertising the position opening. Some institutions tend to write generic ads and then sharpen their criteria afterwards. But in the process, they lose some of the advantages of advertising.

By developing a clear-cut statement of qualities, the committee has already done most of the job of determining how it will evaluate credentials of individuals. A single set of criteria consistently applied throughout the search will serve as a defense against hidden political or personal favoritism that otherwise can invade a process to its detriment.

If time allows, a statement of leadership qualities can be developed in two stages. It is sometimes useful to write a draft statement and circulate it to various constituencies for their critique. Especially if some of their reactions are incorporated into a revised draft, the final version can signal to these constituencies that they indeed have been heard during a crucial part of the process. When stakeholders know that the leadership criteria they helped draft are in fact the criteria used to evaluate candidates, some of the suspicion that often surrounds the necessary confidentiality of the screening process can be dissipated.

A statement of leadership qualities that has involved the constituencies of a college or university can also stimulate those same constituencies in searching for candidates. Asking students, professors, and alumni to help find "a president" is very different from asking their help to find a *particular* president, as described in a clear and compelling statement of leadership criteria.

Samples of effective statements of leadership qualities appear as Exhibit C in the appendix.

---

[1] David Riesman and Judith B. McLaughlin, "The Vicissitudes of the Search Process," *Review of Higher Education*, Summer, 1985 (vol. 8, no. 4), pp. 344–46.

[2] One example of an external and elaborate institutional analysis is that carried out by Carnegie-Mellon University, *The Search for the President, 1989* (Pittsburgh: Carnegie-Mellon University, March 17, 1989).

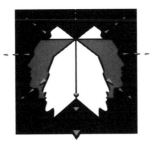

## CHAPTER THREE

# Organizing the Committee

Once the presidential search committee has been formed and its charge from the board received, the committee's work can begin. The committee must plan as many activities and procedures as possible at the start of the process, rather than addressing each new issue as it arises.

## The Committee Chair

The search committee chair embodies the authority of the board and bears responsibility for carrying out the terms of its charge. The chair sets the tone for the committee, directs the discussion, smoothes any ruffled feelings, copes with emergencies. In public institutions, it is the chair who responds to political pressures and demonstrates by his or her impartiality the nonpartisan nature of the search. The chair is the official representative and interpreter of the committee's work to the public, and he or she is the primary liaison between the institution and the candidates. The chair must command respect and remain impartial, discreet, incisive, and sensitive. The chair's actions will shape public perception of the integrity of the process—and, indeed, of the institution itself—throughout the search.

The chair must be prepared to invest a substantial amount of time. Even when an outside consultant is employed, the demands upon the chair for telephone calls, interviews, press conferences, and decisions large and small should not be underestimated. He or she also must be well informed about the entire institution, because the chair's responses to queries may, and in most cases should, be the sole source of public information about the search.

The board, in setting up the search and screening committee(s), also should designate the chair or, at the very least, it should establish specific guidelines on how the committee should choose a chair. Where there are two committees, it is common for a faculty member to chair the search committee and a trustee to chair the selection or screening committee, thus reflecting the relative influence of the two groups in their respective committees.

# Committee Staff and Office

The selection of a president involves a considerable amount of important detail. Committee meetings must be scheduled and often rescheduled. Mailing lists must be prepared. Letters must go out inviting nominations, and advertisements must be placed in appropriate newspapers and journals. Responses must be acknowledged, background data on candidates collected, an efficient filing system established. Interviews must be arranged, travel schedules set up, expenses approved and promptly paid. These functions should not be allowed to burden committee members who donate their time.

The committee requires adequate and responsible staff assistance. In most situations, this means a staff officer or administrative secretary who is discreet and (preferably) can give full time to the assignment for the duration. This person should be someone who knows the institution and who is respected by the various constituencies. Sometimes it is appropriate and possible for an administrative officer to serve the committee on a part-time basis. In either case, varying amounts of clerical help will be needed, especially at times of peak load in correspondence. The staff assistant must be prepared to work closely with the chair and to comply fully with the committee's policies on confidentiality and disclosure.

The committee will need a secure room where files can be safely kept and where the staff officer can receive, sort, and answer mail. Ideally, the room should be secured when unattended but, for the convenience of committee members residing at a distance from the campus, should be accessible when necessary during evening or weekend hours. If it contains or is adjacent to space where the committee can meet, that is an additional advantage.

# Planning the Search

Ordinarily, the board's charge will cede to the committee full authority to design its own procedures. In the public sector, however, it is increasingly common to find specific requirements imposed upon the search process. New Jersey, for example, mandates a six-week period between the first announcement of a vacancy and the closing date for applications. In many states, open-meeting laws ("sunshine" legislation) will guide committee proceedings. And when an executive search agency is employed, the consultant may recommend certain procedures.

Whatever the constraints upon its powers, the committee will find it helpful to map out a comprehensive search plan as its first order of business. Developing a plan has multiple advantages. It ensures that no important step will be overlooked; it allows the establishment of an orderly schedule to which committee members can adapt their own calendars; it specifies and develops consistency among all the search communications; it informs members unfamiliar with academic searches (and this may include the majority of the committee) what to expect; and it helps them anticipate realistically the required commitment of time and effort. It also spares the chair the need to make ad hoc decisions at every turn.

A search plan cannot, of course, be too rigid. The vicissitudes of travel, weather, and other uncertainties will necessitate some flexibility. Nonetheless, systematic preparation at the outset will more than repay the time invested. A comprehensive plan should include, at a minimum, the following elements: agreement on the committee's working rules (including individual attendance obligations), provision for compliance with university personnel policies and applicable legislation, design of a communications plan, arrangements for record keeping, design of budget and timetable, and methods for developing, screening, and interviewing a pool of candidates.

# Committee Procedures

Teams work best in an environment of candor, mutual respect, and informality. The fewer rules, the better. Members who can agree to the courtesies of regular attendance and punctuality, who are prepared to contribute to consensus, and who have confidence that their views are heard and respected will be able to focus on the task without distraction. Guidelines that promote these conditions should be established early. Likewise, guidelines concerning members' prerogatives must be formulated. Who authorizes expenditures, and what costs will be reimbursed? What arrangements are needed for parking? For access to files? What information will be publicly shared? How will conflicts of interest be resolved?

As the committee plans the details of the search, members will anticipate a variety of such procedural questions. Settling them early and recording the decisions in the minutes allows the committee to clear its agenda for the much larger issues to come.

# Compliance With Law and Policy

Because universities need a variety of legal services from time to time, most institutions have established arrangements for providing legal counsel. Similarly, most campuses have designated an administrator—often the personnel director or a member of that staff—to serve as affirmative-action officer. The search committee will benefit from early briefings by the university attorney and the affirmative-action officer. They are key resources.

The university counsel will address federal equal-opportunity legislation, which applies to all programs receiving federal funds, as well as any related state laws. Although most committee members will be generally familiar with the provisions of such legislation, the attorney can describe specifically how these laws apply to the conduct of the search. For publicly supported institutions, the attorney's interpretation of state open-meeting laws will prove invaluable.

The affirmative-action officer will be more specifically concerned with board-mandated personnel policies. Again, the search group will be generally acquainted with these, and if the group includes a trustee with experience on the board's personnel committee (if one exists), that member will be well prepared to interpret the board's intent. The affirmative-action officer can distill from the accumulated experience of many searches specific guidance about reviewing credentials, about interviewing, and about other forms of information gathering.

In colleges that are part of a multicampus system, the search committee also will want to consult a system representative concerning the central office's expectations. Systems vary widely in the degree of influence they exert upon constituent campuses. Some have detailed codes regulating the conduct of searches, while others have only informal—perhaps unwritten—expectations, though even these, if ignored, can create serious embarrassments.

In some states, a designee from the central office serves on each presidential search; in others, expert advice is provided through a professional consultant hired to assist the committee in formulating its search plan or to review the plan after it has been drafted. Further, in some systems a uniform presidential job description applies to all campuses, while in others the trustees, like their counterparts in the private sector, have the opportunity to compose a unique description. Occasionally, system personnel policies apparently unrelated to the presidency may impinge upon the selection—for example, policies related to the award of tenure.

# The Problem of Confidentiality

Candidates for a presidency—a majority of them at least—would prefer that their candidacy be kept confidential. The campus community and the public press, on the other hand, want to know what is going on. The selection of a new president provides a classic example of the conflict between the individual's right to privacy and the public's right to know.

Inevitably, breaches of promised confidentiality and refusals to provide information will cause problems. Thus, every search committee must decide at the start how to handle this complex issue. Public institutions may have fewer choices than independent ones, because virtually every state now has open-meeting or right-to-know legislation. There is great variation, however, in the stringency of such laws. Many states exempt personnel matters from public scrutiny, thus allowing search committees a significant measure of privacy, at least while the search is taking place. (If, however, committee minutes become public documents once the search has ended, they may then be available to the press under right-to-know laws.) Other states, notably Florida, require all state business to be conducted "in the sunshine"—that is, in public view. If sunshine laws allow the use of an executive search organization, the consultant can help to delay or to avoid undesirable disclosures.

Some presidents prefer on principle to have everything out in the open. Others for practical reasons think it preferable. "My candidacy was known to the campus community at the time of my initial visit," writes one private university president. "Thus, I had an opportunity to speak openly to faculty, staff, and students prior to my appointment. I liked it that way."

The major disadvantages of such a procedure are twofold. First, it may reduce the number of top candidates, for the best qualified individuals are sometimes the least inclined to submit themselves to public scrutiny—at least before they are clearly finalists. Indeed, the best people frequently need to be recruited and wooed rather than publicly displayed. Second, publicity jeopardizes the candidate's position or standing in his or her present institution, and public discussion of the merits of various candidates is often embarrassing to those not selected. Because of the prevalence of these views, most presidential searches observe the strictest confidence.

Applicants and nominees will, of course, want to know at the outset whether confidentiality will be maintained. When a promise of confidentiality is given, more is at stake than mere courtesy (although courtesy should not be ignored). Regrettable tales have entered permanently into the lore of presidential searching. One instance, described by Theodore J. Marchese and Jane Fiori Lawrence, concerns a committee member who commented casually that "the dean at Siwash may be interested." A colleague, continued Marchese, "happened to mention it to someone down the hall, who mentioned it on the phone to a friend at Siwash, who mentioned it to that college's president, who brought the dean in on the carpet."[1]

Events of this kind are less likely to occur if a committee is apprised of the possible consequences. No one wants to be responsible for disrupting a career or for frightening off other promising candidates.

A breach of confidentiality can occur in different ways. The most common is by leaks, which seem to be endemic in modern life and particularly in political situations. These occur most frequently where the departure of the last president left a troubled campus, where one or more internal candidates have local supporters or critics, and where an aggressive press is looking for answers. The best one can do is to pledge members of the screening committee to complete secrecy, to announce that the finalists will be brought to the campus for open interviews, to report regularly and frequently on the progress of the search (except for the names of candidates), and to discuss in advance how inquiries should be handled. A sound communication plan is vital to the success of this effort.

Two good rules to follow: (1) The committee should appoint a single spokesperson, in most cases its chair; and (2) the spokesperson should establish early and good working relations with the media.

The composition of the committee, its mandate, the procedures it proposes to follow, and its progress week by week are matters of public interest and should be explained carefully to students, faculty, alumni, and the public. The spokesperson should establish contact with the student newspaper, representatives of the public press, and where interested, with broadcasters for radio and television. One private university committee chair won the cooperation of the media by telling reporters frankly at the beginning of the search that premature public discussion of individual candidates would cause the university to lose some of its best prospects and that he would keep them fully informed of everything except the identification of the candidates.

Of course, disclosure of finalist candidates will necessarily occur if they make a public visit to the campus. Such visits serve valuable purposes. They enable local constituencies to see and size up the candidates, an exercise that is particularly important for faculty and administration. At the same time, they give candidates a chance to appraise the institution and the groups that compose it. If finalists are to be invited for open campus visits, they should understand this expectation early in the search process. In fact, if at any time in the process it is necessary to announce candidate names, candidates should be advised in advance that their identities and biographies will become public. They may prefer to withdraw, and they should, in fairness, be given an opportunity to do so.

Basically, confidentiality requires attention throughout the process. The key to success is to inform all persons involved about the ground rules and not change them unless absolutely necessary.

# Communications and Public Relations

A presidential search offers an unprecedented opportunity to enhance the university's standing among its many constituencies. Interest in the search, although especially intense on campus, will extend well beyond these boundaries, beyond the alumni family, even beyond the local community. Because a president embodies the aspirations of a university and its vision of the future, the selection will be monitored closely by peer institutions, by professional associations, by funding organizations and other benefactors, perhaps by football fans and state legislatures, and most assuredly by the press. Nominations may come from many of these groups, and stories about the search will be read by many more. Before the final choice is announced, thousands will be touched in one way or another by the actions of the search committee. It therefore behooves the committee to prepare for this scrutiny and, more important, to make the most of it.

Doing so requires, at a minimum, keeping all interested parties fully and accurately informed. Here the issue of confidentiality becomes acute. Releasing too much information can embarrass candidates and may result in losing them; releasing too little can offend the many constituents and may invite distrust and rumor-mongering. If the search is not subject to sunshine laws and if the committee has agreed to the principle of confidentiality, then it must decide what information to disclose, when, to whom, and by whom.

The last question—who shall speak for the committee—is straightforward. If several people respond to inquiries, particularly those relating to policy, confusion will inevitably ensue. As suggested earlier, the spokesperson ordinarily will be the committee's chair. All inquiries should be referred to the spokesperson, all correspondence will bear his or her signature, and he or she will speak for the committee on all public occasions.

By demeanor and language, the committee, through its spokesperson, will shape public perceptions of the search and of the university itself. To satisfy the intense curiosity surrounding a presidential search and to promote a sense of inclusion on campus, the committee will find a policy of forthrightness advantageous. All constituencies should be kept informed of the progress of the search, and the information provided should be as complete as possible, consonant with the requirements of confidentiality. Although names and titles will not, of course, be disclosed (unless required by law) statistical data (numbers of applicants and geographic distribution) should pose no problem. General data, rather than specific numbers, usually suffice.

The course of every search is punctuated by a series of decision points that mark the completion of one phase and the start of the next. These provide natural occasions for faculty bulletins, alumni news reports, and press releases summarizing progress. The first such occasion occurs when all members of the search committee have been appointed and have accepted the charge from the board, the next when the board has formulated the presidential qualities it seeks and the committee has devised a recruiting program, and so on until the board makes its selection and announces an appointment.

Communications, which cannot discuss candidates, should be as complete as possible on procedures and progress. Appearing at regular intervals, these bulletins appease the hunger for information and halt the rumor mill. More important, they build a sense of momentum and expectation that ultimately translates into an enthusiastic welcome for the new president.

The pool of applicants represents another news-hungry constituency. They must be kept informed of the status of their candidacy, the progress of the search, and the date when the next committee action will occur. As screening narrows the field, those no longer under consideration need to be promptly informed, while those retained in the pool should receive more complete information about the university, both to keep their interest alive and to enlarge their understanding of what the presidency requires.

To route this information flow, the staff officer must keep meticulous correspondence records and precise minutes of committee decisions. Because the committee's actions may exert a lasting impact on candidates' careers, correspondence deserves to be handled with tact and courtesy. Thoughtless or clumsy treatment of unsuccessful applicants can damage an institution's reputation. Moreover, an unsuccessful candidate may reappear, a few years later, as the winner of a search at a neighboring campus whose friendly cooperation is important. Because the presentation and timing of public information can shape the perceived image of the university, careful planning is essential to the communication program.

# Timetable

Selection committees, like legislatures, tend to start slowly and end in a rush. It is not just that the final deadline seems at first a comfortable distance away; committees frequently underestimate the time required and the cumulative impact of inevitable delays. Therefore, it is important for the committee to set a realistic schedule for itself at the start of its operations. This schedule should allow for the time necessary to organize, to send out letters inviting nominations, to place advertisements and acknowledge replies, to screen the curricula vitae of candidates, to check references and arrange preliminary interviews with perhaps eight to ten individuals and campus visits for the final three to five, to make final checks on the finalists, and to reach agreement on the candidates to be recommended to the board.

The committee will find it a useful technique to work backward from prescribed dates (reporting to the board, naming of the president) to determine when to start the process. In its charge to the committee, the board should have set the date, usually one of its regularly scheduled meetings, at which it expects to take action on the committee's recommendations. This date should be early enough to permit the president-designate to take over from the outgoing incumbent without an interregnum (except in crisis situations). It also should allow for some additional margin of time in case the committee or board cannot agree on a candidate or if the chosen candidate declines to accept.

How long will the search and selection process take? This varies greatly from one institution to the next, depending on the nature of the transition and the point in the academic calendar at which the search takes place. Universities tend to take a longer time than two-year colleges, for example. Public institutions on the whole take less time than private institutions.

The chair of a church-related college search committee, which spent four months reviewing 85 candidates, comments: "In my opinion, a search committee can spend too much time on a search. Deadlines must be established and met." Most committees would be happy if their labors could be limited to four months. The optimal length depends partly on local circumstances and partly on the efficiency of the committee. Four working months (discounting major vacation periods) are probably the minimum for a nationwide, comprehensive search. Five months are preferable and six a good outside limit for a normal search process. *Only in the most unusual circumstances should a search be allowed to extend beyond eight months.* As the search lengthens, the best candidates will be lost to other institutions or will withdraw.

During the search process, the amount of time required from committee members is considerable. Weekly or fortnightly meetings for long periods are not uncommon, though not always necessary. In one community college where the entire seven-member board served as the search committee, members met twice or three times per week for five months. This is an extreme situation, even for such an important task. Because of their experience, executive search consultants can recommend methods to greatly increase efficiency, saving committee members unnecessary expenditure of time while still allowing full, responsible involvement in the process. Exhibit D in the appendix contains a sample timetable.

# The Cost of a Search

Accurately estimating the cost of selecting a new president is difficult. Some institutions include in their cost figures pro rata salaries of administrative officers and staff secretaries, while others list only the more obvious out-of-pocket expenses occasioned by committee travel and bringing candidates to the campus. The time donated by committee members is of course a real, albeit unrecorded, cost to the institution.

Consider the costs involved in a search: one administrative staff member, full-time or part-time; one clerical secretary (and at certain peak periods two); advertising in public media; stationery; postage; filing cabinets; telephone and telefax; committee travel and meals; candidate travel, housing, and meals; and the fees of any outside consultants. Trustees of independent colleges or universities may donate their own travel expenses along with their services, but it is not reasonable to expect other committee members to do so, and it is certainly not desirable to ask candidates to pay their own way.

The appendix (Exhibit E) contains a sample search budget. It cannot be emphasized too strongly that the selection of the new president is so vital to the life of the institution—and the selection of the wrong one potentially so disastrous—that this is no place to risk failure through false economy. After all, the successful candidate will be managing a multimillion dollar operation, and the cost of finding the right person—as opposed to the wrong one—will quickly fade into insignificance.

Some committees are instructed to do whatever is necessary and not to worry about the cost; the college or university will pick up the tab. At the other extreme is the dangerous assumption by the board or by the committee that the job must be done at minimal cost by cutting corners and overworking staff. Most committees will find it more comfortable to calculate in advance a budget of expenses and to know that funds will be sufficient to cover them. If funds are not available, for example, for ten preliminary interviews or for four campus visits by final candidates and their spouses, the program must be tailored accordingly. These numbers, however, come close to being the minimum for a well-conducted search.

# Paperwork and Record Keeping

The normal search and selection process generates a substantial mass of documents. In addition to hundreds of letters and memoranda announcing the vacancy and inviting nominations or applications, the committee will collect documents providing information on from 50 to as many as 300 candidates. For each there needs to be a dossier containing biographical information and correspondence, and for those who survive the early screening process, there will be reports on references and other conversations, telephone calls, and interviews.

Some committees make copies of all documents for each member of the committee, accepting the not inconsiderable cost of doing so and also the very real risk that sensitive and confidential information may inadvertently find its way into the wrong hands. Other committees, for reasons of economy or security, maintain a central office and file to which only members and staff have access and where they can do their homework. This is manageable where much of the screening is done by campus members of the committee, but under most circumstances it imposes an additional burden on already overworked trustee members.

All search committees will want to invest a good deal of time and effort in securing qualified minority and women candidates. Regulations regarding equal opportunity and affirmative action require committees subject to such regulations to demonstrate by the record, if challenged, the legitimacy of their actions. The best policy is to maintain full and complete records of committee activities and decisions. This record should include minutes of meetings showing decisions respecting the status of candidates (but it is necessary only to note process and outcomes; detailed minutes of deliberations are not required). The record should show how wide the net had been cast and how many candidates were women and members of minority groups. Normally, full committee records must be retained for inspection for one year after completion of the search.

The need for a complete record of official actions also is important for keeping the search process on track. Consideration of many candidates over many weeks and months breeds confusion. Memories become dim or erratic. Ultimately, the record will prove to be a useful guide when the time comes to seek a successor president or when the next history of the university is written.

When the committee has completed the foregoing arrangements, it will be ready to design the more substantial elements of the search plan—the methods of developing, screening, and interviewing qualified candidates. Now the committee will want to review its charge once again, with particular attention to the presidential leadership qualities it has developed.

---

[1] Theodore J. Marchese and Jane Fiori Lawrence, *The Search Committee Handbook*, (Washington, D.C.: American Association for Higher Education 1987), p. 14.

CHAPTER FOUR

# Developing a Pool of Candidates

Once the criteria for the presidency have been approved and committee procedures established, the next step is to develop a roster of candidates who match the criteria. Now the search committee will shift into high gear. Recruiting is an active process which, at its best, enlists the efforts of many people, both on campus and off. The committee's task will be to orchestrate these efforts while focusing attention on the leadership criteria.

## Scope of the Search

How wide a net should the committee cast? This varies with local circumstances—the mission of the campus, its needs, traditions, and aspirations.

On very few occasions, a board of trustees, its chair, or the outgoing president has a handpicked candidate ready and available—usually an internal candidate who has been groomed for the job. The concept and practice of succession planning is common in the corporate world and occasionally seems to be acceptable in private independent higher education. The concept of shared governance in higher education requires, however, that considerable care be given to ensure that key constituencies share trustee enthusiasm for the practice and the candidate.

Slightly less extreme is the situation where the president must be a member of a religious order or denomination—a requirement that can sharply limit the number of possible candidates.

Unless restricted by charter or tradition, most universities will seek the advantages of a comprehensive search. These advantages are substantial. Trustees want not just a competent chief executive but the best match for their particular institution at this point in its history. They want the individual who most completely displays the leadership qualities they have carefully chosen. The president's influence on the campus is too pervasive and too far-reaching to justify settling for anything less than the best person available.

The best person available may be female or black or Hispanic or a member of another minority. In the past decade, representatives of these groups have risen to the top ranks of academic management, where they have shown incontrovertibly that leadership has neither gender nor ethnic restrictions. Many members of formerly excluded groups have now attained levels of experience and accomplishment that qualify them as presidential candidates. One of the advantages of a comprehensive search is the opportunity to tap these reservoirs of talent.

Still another benefit of the broad search is the involvement of greater numbers of people. If invited to submit nominations or to suggest other possible nominators, faculty, students, alumni and local citizens gain a sense of participation and a stake in the outcome. Requests to educators, foundation officers, and other distinguished citizens will arouse their interest in the institution, increase their knowledge of it, and, if done astutely, enhance its reputation.

Professional search consultants confirm the wisdom of casting a wide net. Because talent is broadly dispersed throughout the academic and other populations, it is impossible to predict where the best candidates will be found or how they will present themselves. No single route leads to them. The most productive searches do not limit themselves to a single means; they use all available means, and use them aggressively.

The foregoing advocates selection from a large pool of candidates. Large, however, does not mean indiscriminate nor does it mean increasing the size of the pool for the sake of size alone. If the leadership criteria are well drawn, they will encourage more qualified candidates who know by the careful wording that the search is a serious one. They will also discourage some (not all, unfortunately!) clearly unqualified candidates who apply for any new position, especially if the criteria are vague.

Numbers can lie, as everyone knows. Two hundred candidates are not necessarily better than one hundred. An institution is, after all, looking for a single individual. What really counts is attracting 15–20 strong, plausible candidates who include among them 8–10 semifinalists and 3–5 finalists who are so impressive that the board will have genuine difficulty in choosing among them. To reach those final numbers, large universities may attract more than 150 candidates. A comprehensive institution or one with national identification may attract 80–100. Smaller, especially more specialized or regional institutions, might develop a pool half as large but, if clear about the leadership criteria, could easily have a better ratio of good finalists to total applicants than larger institutions.

One rule of thumb should guide the search: a pool can always be reduced, but it is more difficult to increase. A candidate who is in the pool can always be rejected; a potential candidate who is not in the pool cannot even be considered. In general, a larger, more diverse pool is always to an institution's advantage.

# Sources of Names

There are various ways of developing a pool of candidates. Most committees employ more than one; a few use them all.

The time-honored method is to announce the vacancy (by press release, notice in the campus news bulletin, story in the alumni magazine) and to write letters to a variety of individuals inviting them to nominate suitable candidates. Broadcast invitations can go to faculty, students, and alumni. Individual letters should be sent to selected educators, foundation officers, church leaders, government officials, heads of educational organizations, and selected friends of the university. Not to be overlooked are presidents and trustees of peer institutions. Indeed, one of the search committee's responsibilities is to decide which are the peer institutions for this purpose. The extent of the mailing will depend on the national or regional character of the institution, the availability of funds, and the degree of concern on the part of committee members to canvass the field.

Private colleges and universities tend to put more emphasis and value than do public institutions on nominations from people who know the college or university. Many have reported that nominations by knowledgeable individuals were by far their best source of candidates. Exhibit F in the appendix contains a typical letter inviting nominations. The information accompanying these letters should make clear that each institution is an affirmative action/equal opportunity employer. Exhibits G and H are examples of letters acknowledging nominations and informing nominees that their names have been submitted.

A second and concurrent approach is to advertise. There was a time when presidents, like ministers, were expected to receive "a call" to a new post. To apply for the position was considered quite improper. It is still true that some of the best individuals—often the very best—will not apply, either because they consider it presumptuous or because they are happily situated where they are. Many, however, use an associate to nominate them, so that they are in fact applying. The difference between nominations and applications is therefore not as great as it may seem. Excellent candidates do respond to advertising though their proportion may not be as great as from other sources. In any case, the legal requirements of equal opportunity/affirmative action encourage, though they do not require, public solicitation of candidates.

The most widely used vehicles for public notices are the *Chronicle of Higher Education,* the *New York Times* (especially the Sunday edition), the *Wall Street Journal* (for national audiences), and local newspapers. The *Chronicle* seems to be the most effective. The *New York Times* and the *Wall Street Journal* may be effective in some cases, but they are expensive. In addition, many committees make selective use of notices in educational journals, church or denominational bulletins, and publications with specialized audiences. In most cases, all advertisements combined generate a considerable number of applicants. Unless a deadline is mandated, advertisements need not put an absolute deadline on the date by which applications *must* be received. Occasionally, the best suggestions arrive a few days after a closing date and might be excluded by too strict a cutoff.

The third avenue is a refinement or specialized form of public advertising. Special publications and organizations have been created to assist in locating women, blacks, and other minority candidates. The number of these publications has increased in recent years as a result of federal and state legislation. Some may be helpful in reaching diverse candidates. A list of names and addresses of agencies from which help can be sought to make certain that equal opportunity is being promoted is included in the appendix as Exhibit I.

Finally, executive search firms are in business to help organizations to find personnel. Their role and value were discussed in detail in Chapter 1. Some colleges and universities have found such firms useful in providing names of excellent candidates. Those designed as a nonprofit, tax-exempt service to higher education, such as AGB's Presidential Search Consultation Service (PSCS), are familiar with the academic world and therefore in a position to advise about who is available and who would be particularly suitable for an institution, given its mission and educational management needs.

There is no value in a large roster of candidates unless the right candidates are included. The sources outlined here may produce the right candidates, but there is no guarantee, of course. Committees, boards, alumni, and faculty should act energetically, writing or preferably telephoning well-placed friends of the institution and individuals who ought to be on the list. They should urge others on campus to do the same. To the extent the statement of leadership criteria is compelling and widely known, it is more likely that these groups will become involved. Finding the best candidates requires an active—even aggressive—*recruiting* effort. There is no substitute.

# The Reluctant Candidate

It cannot be emphasized too strongly that many of the best candidates are unlikely to apply and need to be courted. These individuals normally occupy good positions, and while they might be enticed to go elsewhere, they are in no hurry to do so. They often have enough self-confidence to expect that jobs will be seeking them rather than the reverse. The ideal candidate is one who has substantial achievements and who asks himself or herself, "Shall I stay here longer or go on to a different kind of challenge?"

Committees sometimes assume that anyone—well, almost anyone—would be flattered to be asked to head their college or university, and therefore fail to recognize the need to sell the position. This is often a delicate and sometimes drawn-out process. Sometimes committees create their own obstacles, such as asking individuals who have been nominated whether they are interested in applying for the job. A much better approach is to ask if the committee can interest them in the position or, if the individuals look like first-rate candidates, whether the committee might talk with them about possible candidates. Out of this conversation might develop a person's own interest in being considered. Strong candidates are people who enjoy accomplishing things. Committees should emphasize the opportunities for accomplishment on the campus and the advantages of rising to the challenge.

This point is well stated by Donald E. Fouts in his article, "Picking a President the Business Way." "The business search begins," he writes, "with the basic assumption that the ideal candidate is functioning successfully in his or her present position, not actively seeking new employment and will probably not respond to advertisements or form-letter invitations to apply. Second, it is assumed that the search consultant has a responsibility to aggressively seek out such prospects and 'sell' them on the advantages of candidacy. Third, it is assumed that there is usually a direct relationship between the quality of the candidate and the amount of effort required to interest him or her in the position."[1]

This may overstate the case, but it would be difficult to overstate the need for the personal approach and for courting likely candidates, both at this beginning stage and later when the committee is nearing the moment of truth.

One caveat: Some possible candidates simply want to be courted. They really are not interested in being seriously considered. A committee should beware spending too much time on candidates who seem interesting because of their accomplishments and prestige but who also do not show some real interest in the position.

# The Inside Candidate

Because inside candidates are known to committee members and because they have their strong advocates and quite possibly equally strong critics on campus, they present a special case for the committee.

If one or more strong internal candidates exists, and particularly if one obvious choice who matches the leadership criteria stands out, it is tempting to short-circuit an elaborate search process. It will be tempting to save time, money, and energy. Unless prohibited by law or by institutional bylaws, there is no obvious legal obstacle to promoting the provost, dean, or vice president without further ado.

There are, however, certain dangers and disadvantages in so quick a decision. The insider is likely to have worked long enough with the departing president perhaps to have adopted his or her style or philosophy of education and administration. This may not be what the college or university needs at that juncture. Further, the institution loses the public-relations value of a public search and the internal value of enhanced trust and goodwill among trustees, faculty, and students. And then there is the danger that the inside candidate may not be so much of a local hero as informal reports suggest. In particular, hasty replacement of one white male by another may invite criticism. Sensitivity to constituent concerns must be high on the agenda. The search committee would be well advised to investigate with utmost care the candidate's true standing. This is a task an outside consultant can often perform better than anyone on the inside.

If the committee decides, as most committees do, to carry through an open search, it must handle the inside candidate(s) with care. To tell internal candidates that they will be treated like everyone else is easy; that indeed is the way they ought to be treated and in most cases will want to be treated. But their supporters will be eager, and campus politics being what they are, may make special efforts on their behalf. Often, too, it is more difficult to maintain confidentiality about internal candidates. The analysis of leadership needs will prove especially valuable in these circumstances. All candidates—internal applicants no less than others—must qualify in light of these criteria. Incorporating the adopted statement of qualities into the board's charge to the committee and stressing its importance as the search begins will keep attention on the criteria rather than on individuals. If insiders do appear in the applicant pool, they should be evaluated (as promised) just like everyone else.

A strong inside candidate can also jeopardize the outside search. People who might normally be interested may suspect that the search is a charade and therefore decline to be considered. The committee may have to make an extra effort to convince outsiders that the search is wide open and on the level.

# Correspondence

Preoccupation with screening and with the resulting short list of candidates leads many committees to neglect rank-and-file candidates. Sometimes, months will go by without any communication from committee to candidates, who are concerned about making potential career, location, income, and family adjustments. A sound communications plan, designed before the flood of correspondence rises, will avert this discourtesy.

It is important not only as a matter of courtesy to acknowledge all applications, nominations, inquiries, and letters of support, but also to maintain communication with candidates, nominators, and others actively involved. Sensitive and personal treatment, even for those not in the running, in the long run will contribute to the reputation of the institution. After all, many candidates will be presidents somewhere someday—perhaps even in the same city or state. They should recall how well they were handled in your search, rather than carry unhappy memories about your institution.

---

[1] Donald E. Fouts, "Picking a President the Business Way," *AGB Reports* (vol. 19, no. 1, January/February 1977), p. 8.

## CHAPTER FIVE

# Screening and Initial Checks

As names and files of candidates accumulate in response to advertisements and invitations, the work of screening begins. Just how much work will be involved depends on the size of the pool, the mandate to the committee and the design of the committee's internal processes.

The purpose of screening is to identify a limited and manageable number of likely candidates from the longer roster of proposed names. The screening process is apt to stretch out over considerable time unless limits are set in advance and procedures are efficient. Some committees choose to spread out the process over one or two months. Others conduct the initial screening in one or two days.

In general, it is better to look at a candidate pool in its entirety and in a relatively compact time period rather than evaluating candidates as they come in. Committee judgments may shift, and initial evaluations tend to be more critical than later ones.

The committee must make certain preliminary decisions, however. What should be the size of the eventual "select list"? Precisely who shall do the screening? How extensive should be the committee's investigation of candidates? Some committees will be instructed to undertake preliminary screening only, with a second phase assigned to another committee or even assumed by the board itself. Other committees will have a mandate to continue screening until a handful of first-rate individuals remains. The amount of information on which decisions are made will increase with each phase. Some committees find that considering the screening process as three phases works well. In the first phase the list is reduced to 15–25, in the second to 8–10, and in the third to the top candidates the committee recommends to the board.

The committee can make the first reduction fairly quickly on the basis of standard biographical data. Information from references and from the candidates may be necessary for the second reduction, or the committee can rely on the written materials alone, if they are of high quality. For instance, if the leadership criteria have been made available to candidates, committees can ask whether resumes reflect the match between the candidates's credentials and the leadership qualities. A letter discussing the relation of the resume to the leadership criteria is particularly helpful. Interviews may also be scheduled before the final list is recommended to the board.

As in almost all matters pertaining to the search and selection process, committees should adopt procedures suited to their situations. Good and bad practices abound, and the purpose of any procedure should be to help committees adopt the first and avoid the second. Therefore, the following sections recommend procedures that have proved successful in many circumstances, but they should be regarded as general guidelines and not as straightjackets.

# Who Does the Screening

There are various ways of dividing up the work of screening. The first is not to divide it up at all but to insist that every member of the committee read every dossier. Some committees believe quite strongly that this is the only proper way, but it means a large investment of working hours. As the chair of one community college search committee reports: "Screening of about 130 candidates for a 14-member search committee takes far too much time. There should be a better way, but I cannot see how to do it and still involve all the necessary 'publics' to their satisfaction."

A second method divides the main committee into teams, each of which reads and rates its share of the dossiers. The subcommittees then report their tentative conclusions, which are adopted by the committee as a whole unless some member questions a decision to eliminate a candidate—in which case the candidate is kept on the active list. This system works quite well, especially where mutual trust exists among the committee members. Occasionally, someone will feel uneasy that different teams may be using different standards of judgment, but a uniform rating system, based on the leadership criteria and approved by the committee in advance, should provide a fair measure of consistency. If anxiety lingers, the chair can review all selected dossiers to ensure that they conform to the criteria. Clearly to be avoided is a situation in which one committee uses one set of criteria and another committee a different set.

A third route is the special screening committee. Some boards of trustees establish advisory committees of faculty, students, and staff and assign the preliminary screening to these committees. A variation is to create a special screening committee or subcommittee composed of the faculty, staff, and student members of the search committee on the assumption that these people have more time than trustees for the onerous work of sifting curricula vitae. Ordinarily, they also have readier access to the documents normally housed on campus.

Some observers of the search and screening process argue strongly that one or more trustees always ought to be involved in screening, because it is trustees who will make the final selection. Finally, some committees use outside consultants to conduct the necessary screening. This saves the committee time and trouble and is likely to be done more professionally. Consultants can be especially helpful at the stage of initial screening. One very good method is to combine professional and committee screening at all levels. This builds in an objective "second opinion" and allows the committee to focus on candidates members judge differently—often very promising candidates. In any case, the committee must be involved in the final screening.

A sense of teamwork is important to any good process. Without it, the committee's final recommendations to the board may lack conviction or be based on the wrong kinds of compromises. With it, candidates will emerge who have wide support among many constituencies—a good basis for a successful presidency.

# How Extensive an Investigation

Determining how aggressively the committee should seek data on candidates is a delicate matter. The charge to the committee should provide guidance for this activity. In every case, the committee should study all the documents applicants or nominators submit. These constitute the basic dossier for each candidate. For some, the information will be skimpy. Should the committee seek more biographical information? Should it engage in telephone conversations with candidates?

Some boards of trustees are quite clear on what the committee should not do. For example, some boards prohibit the screening committee from writing to or telephoning references or communicating directly with candidates, stipulating that such inquiries should be left to the selection committee. Most boards, however, are quite prepared to have the committee seek the necessary biographical data and collect judgments about the candidates. Indeed, it is difficult to see how committees can do an adequate job of screening unless they seek fairly complete information on each candidate.

All public notices calling attention to the vacancy should request respondents to send a curriculum vitae along with the application. If they fail to send sufficient information, the committee's staff member or secretary should request whatever is needed. A letter from the applicant discussing the match between the leadership criteria and the applicant's attainments also can be valuable.

In the case of nominees, the situation is a little more delicate. Some will not be worth much of the committee's time; some will never be interested; some will; and some may become interested if approached in the right way. To write and ask whether an individual is interested and, if so, to send biographical material is to risk losing at the very start some of those who ultimately may become most attractive. If the nominator has not proffered sufficient information, the committee can ask for more, can check the standard reference sources, and can make inquiries of third parties who presumably know the individual. Often the nominee is not aware that he or she has been nominated. In some cases, of course, the nominees know that they have been nominated, and there is no reason not to communicate directly with them.

How should the biographical data be presented to the committee? Some committees—more in the public sector than in the private—insist that all candidates fill out a standard form. This has the merit of providing comparable data on all candidates and thereby making comparisons among candidates much easier. But it is likely to be a barrier to the reluctant or sophisticated candidate. Other committees prefer to leave the presentation of personal information to the individual, believing that they learn something about that individual by the way in which he or she writes the information.

A compromise between the two methods allows candidates to present their data in their own way, after which the secretary or staff member to the committee summarizes the salient points on a standard form, which then serves as a cover to the curriculum vitae. However, this is often more work than is really necessary, as each committee member will want to make his or her own notes on the candidate's material.

# References—How Valuable

It is pointless—and possibly disadvantageous—to request references as part of the initial application. Applicants who wish their candidacy to remain confidential will not supply them. Candidates who wish to explore the position more fully before committing themselves—often some of the more attractive ones—may actually be deterred from inquiring if references are demanded at the outset. In any case, letters of reference attached to the application are of very little value. Written for the eyes of the applicant as well as those of the prospective employer, they are unlikely to present an objective appraisal of strengths and weaknesses. References with whom the committee corresponds can occasionally be quite informative, but in an increasingly litigious society, they may skirt honesty. On the whole, most searches do not rely heavily on written evaluations.

Conversations on the telephone can be much more revealing. People will say more than they will write. They respond to specific questions. Their inflections and hesitations in expressing their views can sometimes provide information more valuable than their actual words.

Checking out candidates by telephone can become a problem to the committee if a strategy is not carefully planned. By no means should individual committee members take off on their own and call upon friends on other campuses. This can be disastrous. The division of labor in screening candidates needs to be established and approved, so that the committee's time is spent discussing what is learned rather than wasted in bickering over the authority of a committee member to make the inquiry. One way to avoid trouble is to authorize a few members, perhaps the chair among them, to make the calls. Because people respond more honestly to friends and acquaintances, however, there are some advantages in capitalizing on personal connections when this can be done without endangering confidentiality.

Essentially, committee members must agree on what should be asked. Some committees prefer a standard format or set of questions, and certainly telephone conversations should be shaped by an agreed-upon framework. In general, a laundry list of questions, asked unvaryingly for each candidate regardless of background, produces dry and formal replies. A better approach is to ask questions about the same issues for each candidate but to tailor the questions themselves to make them individually applicable. The leadership criteria provide this scaffold; references can be asked whether the candidate displays the necessary qualities, and the caller can request examples. Different candidates raise different questions in the minds of committee members. It is not only appropriate, but also desirable, to ask whether Mr. X really has the strength to stand up for unpopular decisions and whether Ms. Y is genuinely concerned about academic issues.

Checking references by telephone requires considerable skill—more skill than some committee members are likely to possess. An experienced consultant can help at this point, although some committee involvement is desirable. Checking references is a powerful way to develop a personal "feel" for candidates, and committee members should seize this advantage as much as possible.

In telephoning references, confidentiality often is an important consideration. If the individuals do not want their candidacy publicly known, especially in their present place of employment, the committee must honor this request. In addition, references must not be sought from people whose participation would reveal the candidate's interest in another position. Where it is appropriate to proceed, the inquirer should ask the reference to respect the confidential nature of the inquiry. Where the individual is not yet a candidate, this fact must be made clear in any communication with a third party.

# Types of References and Their Timing

In general, it helps to divide reference checks into three phases. In the first phase, it is sufficient to speak only to people suggested by the candidate. When a candidate is promoted to the short or semifinalist list, this good news should be accompanied by a request for several references who can discuss the candidate's accomplishments in relation to the leadership criteria. True, these will be friends and supporters. But the references chosen, how they address the leadership criteria, and of course, what they say about specific experiences can tell the committee a great deal about a candidate. In this phase, the committee refrains from contacting other references—even obvious ones—to respect the candidate's desire for confidentiality.

In the second phase, the committee may contact additional references, including most of those who were out of bounds in the first phase. If candidate permission is no longer sought (some committees still seek it as a courtesy), the committee should be sure to inform the candidate in advance about who is to be contacted. Often the best sources in this phase are individuals mentioned by references in the first phase.

In the final phase, all restrictions are off and candidates should be so advised. Anyone may—indeed, should—be contacted whose opinions about or experience with the candidate are germane. The candidate need no longer be advised about who is contacted.

The first phase covers the select group of eight to ten candidates and should be completed before initial interviews. The second and third phases cover only finalist candidates as they advance in the process.

# Preliminary Interviews

How soon should committees start interviewing candidates? As we have noted, most committees do not make direct contact with candidates early in the search. The conventional procedure is to postpone interviews until the screening process has reduced the roster to the semifinalist list.

Some committees have found that a few early interviews with apparently strong candidates can be highly educational to the committee. Such interviews enable them to focus more clearly on what they seek and to appraise more realistically the paper credentials of the candidates. However, it may be that more emphasis on development of the leadership criteria would obviate the educational value of these early interviews and avoid the confusion that results when some candidates (of varying quality) are interviewed and others are not.

In certain situations, such as when a candidate needs to be persuaded to consider the job, the opportunity to become acquainted and to exchange ideas can make a critical difference. Communication by telephone or mail also can be effective if it is frequent enough and continues to add appealing information and perspectives. Remember, however, that the interest aroused by an early interview is easily dissipated by long delays. Interviews normally are most helpful when scheduled toward the end of the search process. But contact by letter and particularly by phone is necessary throughout the search.

# Rating Systems

The product of the screening process is the semifinalist list. During screening, candidates are sorted into different groups. Fairly standard classifications are (1) prime candidates, (2) possibly worth further consideration, (3) not qualified, and (4) deferred for further information. Some committees will set aside for special consideration inside candidates, although this is generally a bad practice. Committees operating under sunshine laws may find it expedient to be more diplomatic in the statement of their ratings than committees that meet in private.

Some committees develop elaborate rating schedules or forms with weighted values for different features of the candidates' professional and personal qualifications. At their worst, these methods tend to make ratings rather mechanical. The advice of John A. Dunn, Jr., associate vice president of Tufts University and staff officer for its 1976 search committee, is worth considering. "Avoid complex candidate rating systems; the good candidates will surface. Getting through 400 or so candidates is a major job. We formed three 'teams' and rated candidates numerically 1-2-3-4. The top 30 or 40 surfaced on everyone's list."

Reliance on the leadership criteria is an essential element at all stages in candidate screening. In the initial stages, focusing on the global characteristics of the criteria, scoring on a 1-2-3 or yes-maybe-no basis, makes the task manageable. After reducing the list to 20–30 names, the committee should read all dossiers closely, emphasizing the specifics of the leadership criteria and using a detailed rating form. It is especially important for all members to read in detail the dossiers of the more select group. It is never good practice to use detailed, quantitative rating forms and sum the ratings of all evaluators to determine the best candidates. Detailed, quantitative evaluations, when linked to the leadership criteria, can be very helpful to individual committee members as they assess their own evaluations, but they should be used only for that purpose.

Ranking or grouping candidates really is a continuous process from the first rating of early applications to final agreement on the select list. In efforts to speed the process, committees will sometimes make snap judgments and end up shortchanging themselves. Committees should be careful, however, not to rank candidates until all the evidence, including interviews, is in. The issue is not merely that candidates deserve thoughtful consideration—after all, their future careers are involved—but also that the standards and insights of committee members change as the search proceeds.

Frederick Bolman in *How College Presidents Are Chosen* quotes a dean's statement calculated to make committees think twice. "The man whom we finally selected as president started out as a little-known name near the bottom of our secondary list. Because of repeated references by outsiders, his name began to work its way upward on the secondary list until finally it was at the top. Then it was placed at the bottom of our 'number one' list. He continued to get extraordinarily glowing recommendations. As a result, his name continued to move up. Finally, he and one other man were invited to the campus for an interview. In the end, he was selected." This kind of dramatic change occurs infrequently, but committee procedures should allow it to happen.

# Two Cautions

First, stay constantly in touch with candidates. Keep them informed of their status. They should not be left in the dark for long periods. One president criticizes the process by which he was selected: "The length of time in evaluating candidates was too great. There were long periods without any indication from the selection committee of their progress. Stated deadlines for providing information were not met."

Some committees write polite rejection letters as soon as candidates are rated below the "well qualified" or "possibly qualified" rankings. Others prefer to keep all candidacies alive until the end. Either way, the committee owes it to the candidates and to its own success to stay in touch with candidates and to give them some notion of where they stand. Included in the appendix as Exhibit K is a letter to candidates who no longer are being considered.

Second, be sure to make written records of all oral communications with candidates and references and of all committee decisions. With hundreds of candidates, confusion can develop, and over several months memories grow dim. The committee will wish to establish early which materials to add routinely to individual files and which ones individual members may retain as personal evaluative notes to transmit orally. Where a search committee recommends candidates to the board, evidence for the recommendations may be required. But not all such evidence must necessarily be included as written committee records in individual files.

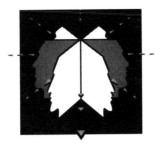

## CHAPTER SIX

# Interviewing Candidates

Screening candidates, chiefly on the basis of their written credentials, is the first step in sorting through the pool. Interviewing those who have survived is the second. No committee that knows its business will nominate candidates for the presidency of the institution without having seen and talked with them face-to-face, and no board worth its salt will appoint anyone sight unseen.

## A Risky Business

First-hand impressions in an interview can be misleading. Some candidates may turn on the charm and dazzle the committee with a brilliant, beguiling performance. Other candidates, either by temperament or because they prefer to conceal part of their past, will appear more reticent. Still others will not make an overwhelming first impression, but will grow on a committee as their true strengths gradually reveal themselves.

Interviewing is a fine art that not everyone possesses by nature or experience, and most committee members will profit from a little professional guidance. A training session or a practice run under the expert supervision of a consultant will greatly improve the performance of interviewing teams. This is important because the results of the interviews often are decisive.

One perceptive administrator who served as chief staff member to a university selection committee writes: "I have some sense that committees can get into more trouble in the interviewing stage than in the screening stage. We tried to avoid this by asking our director of personnel to conduct a briefing session for the interviewing committees on how to interview. Everyone (especially successful people like trustees) thinks he is a good interviewer. And very few are." Corporate executive trustees often are impatient with such educational briefings, but they should be encouraged to participate nonetheless. If only because state and federal laws require interviewers to avoid certain questions, everyone benefits from a thorough briefing on these and related matters.

Most committee members say the interview indeed is decisive. Not only was it "the most fruitful part of the process," says one board chair, "it also led to dramatic changes in comparative rankings." "We continued to be surprised," says another chair, "by the magnitude of the discrepancies that existed between images formed on the basis of applications and recommendations and images generated on the basis of direct contact with candidates."

Most committees use the interview as a means to arrive at the finalist list by screening out candidates who have survived the first and second rounds. Although some reference checking should precede the interview, final reviews of competence and suitability, through more extensive reference checking on work, management style, and track record, will follow the initial interview. These checks should be increasingly rigorous as the field is narrowed and individual candidates advance.

# A Two-Way Street

The interview is usually the first face-to-face contact between the candidate and members of the committee—after weeks of correspondence, telephone conversations, and waiting. The impressions gained on both sides are often crucial. Committees must remember that the candidate is judging the college or university just as the committee is appraising the candidate.

The best candidates, as we have noted, often are skeptical but interested and want more information. They will be influenced by the way they are treated, the questions they are asked and how theirs are answered, and the setting and atmosphere of the interview. Committee members have the difficult role of being both questioners and salespeople.

Thoughtful candidates will ask how the institution operates and about its problems and prospects. They may have conducted a surprising amount of research on the institution on their own. They will be curious about the extent to which trustees, faculty, and others understand problems and prospects and the degree of their commitment to the institution. If the institution is a public college or university, they will want to know about the political climate and the influence of the governor's office, the legislative committee on education, and the budget system. Candidates may want to supplement their impressions with first-hand analyses of interinstitutional cooperation or conflict. (See Exhibit L for questions candidates are likely to ask and committee members should be prepared to discuss.)

Candidates should have received extensive information about the institution before the interview. Newly elected presidents regularly complain that they lacked the truly relevant information about the people and problems of an institution before they had to make a decision about the job. Examples of information to supply to candidates before interviews appear in Exhibit M.

From the committee's side of the table, the interview is a golden opportunity to sell the college or university. This task is made up partly of presenting information, partly of setting the atmosphere, and partly of establishing the attitude. The chair plays the lead role, and is responsible for putting the candidate at ease, for directing the course of the discussion, for curbing irrelevancies, for stopping the undiplomatic committee member, and for easing an embarrassing situation by humor or a change of topic.

Rather than resenting inquiries by candidates, committees should welcome them. Requests for information or frank opinions should be treated as an expression of interest, not an intrusion. Often the failure to provide full information to the candidate is accidental. Full disclosure and complete candor always help more than they hinder. After all, the purpose of the search, ultimately, is to find a fit between a particular individual and the needs of the institution. That fit can be achieved only in an atmosphere of honesty.

# How Many Interviews

It would appear that most committees interview from five to fifteen candidates in the first round, although some interview as many as thirty. The number will be determined in part by the nature and extent of the screening process. One private college that interviewed thirty candidates concluded in its review of the selection process that a few well-placed telephone calls would have enabled it to cut the number of interviews in half.

The temptation is to skimp on interviews for reasons of cost, the amount of time and energy required of committee members, and the danger of raising false expectations on the part of candidates. This argument is understandable but unpersuasive.

We can only reiterate that the choice of the next president justifies whatever investment of money may be required. Money and committee time are not unlimited but the importance of the job justifies whatever output is necessary. Interviews do raise hopes and may be misinterpreted by candidates and their friends. This is a risk, but a far less serious one than eliminating the right individual or staying with the wrong one on the basis of written credentials alone.

Where doubts or differences of opinion exist among committee members, it becomes all the more important to see the candidates. In general, interviewing a slate of seven to nine semifinalist candidates produces the best results. It also is best to interview the candidates during one continuous time period. Seven to nine candidates can be interviewed in two days, a reasonable time requirement for committee members.

# Scheduling Interviews

There is no standard rule about where interviews should take place. Some institutions send teams to interview candidates on their home ground. Although this may be more revealing than interviews held elsewhere, it is potentially more embarrassing to the candidates. Although, once again, cost should not be a determining factor, this method can be expensive unless the search committee has access to free air transport. This practice should, therefore, be employed only with great caution and generally should not be used in the first round of interviews. In no case should such interviews take the candidate by surprise or be arranged without the candidate's full participation.

Confidentiality is best served by selecting neutral sites—for example, an off-campus hotel, a trustee's office, or a corporate meeting room. Community colleges are more inclined to hold interviews on campus. For many of them, confidentiality is less important then convenience, and in some states everything is out in the open under the requirements of sunshine laws.

The physical setting of the interviews should be appropriate, tasteful, and pleasant. Candidates' expenses should be covered. Spouses are not customarily included at the first interview, but if invited, their expenses should also be paid. Arrangements should be made for overnight accommodations, if necessary. Some thought needs to be given to the room in which the interviews take place and to the placing of chairs and tables to create an informal and, so far as possible, relaxed atmosphere. Interior rooms with no windows become oppressive to candidates and committees alike. If candidates are to be kept waiting, a pleasant place to wait is important.

Although it is tempting to crowd interviews close together to save time, interviews should not be rushed. One-hour interviews are apt to be perfunctory; it is better to allot two to three hours for each individual. With such a schedule, three (or at most four) interviews are enough for one day. Interviewing is hard work, and after several hours one inevitably grows weary. Some break between interviews will give committee members a chance to make notes, but committee members should not discuss candidates until all have been interviewed.

The schedule of interviews should be arranged so that candidates do not encounter one another. Even where the semifinalist list is public knowledge, candidates should be kept out of one another's way. On one private college campus, candidates were whisked from one faculty house to another to prevent them from meeting. In another situation, all candidates were invited to the campus on the same day, repeatedly bumped into one another, and reported the process "demeaning and degrading." In still another situation, several candidates were brought together at the same time for purposes of interviewing and "social interaction." At least one participant found this method clumsy and confusing and would have preferred more emphasis on individual treatment. We concur.

Committee members should never lose sight of their two-fold purpose: to learn about the candidate and to sell the institution and its opportunities. This is especially urgent when some candidates remain uncommitted or only marginally interested.

# The Interviewing Team

Who should do the interviewing? The whole committee, if possible. For reasons of convenience or expense, some committees set up more than one team of interviewers, but this establishes the risk that members of one team will react to candidates differently from members of another team. Having the entire committee involved in each interview makes consensus easier to reach and leaves a better impression on candidates. It permits each constituency represented on the committee to get answers to its concerns, and it avoids the danger of multiple teams becoming advocates for "their" candidates.

Avoid interviews by individual committee members. Although this practice sometimes is specifically forbidden by committee rules, a committee member occasionally will be in the vicinity of a candidate and may be encouraged by other members to seize the opportunity. Such an interview may be helpful but should only be obtained with the knowledge and approval of the committee. It should not be used as a substitute for an interview by the entire committee or one of its teams.

Some committees rely on professional consultants to conduct preliminary interviews. The outside consultant has certain advantages in talking with candidates. As a professional personnel officer, the consultant brings the special skills important to good interviewing. As a person of wide experience in higher education, he or she is better prepared than the average committee member to relate personality traits to institutional needs and problems. And as a third party, the consultant is in a strategic position to interpret the institution's situation and opportunities to the candidate more realistically and persuasively than most committee members. For the same reason, a consultant can more easily and gracefully gauge the candidate's interest.

However, there is a danger in relying only on a consultant's interviews. No individual is without bias, and committees bring more than one point of view to bear. Furthermore, at various points in the process, the committee members, as representatives of the institution, must begin to assume "ownership" of the candidates, and they cannot do so unless they meet them. Even when a consultant is employed, candidates eventually should meet the committee.

# What Questions to Ask

Committee members should know a great deal about a candidate by the time he or she comes for an interview, and the members should have the full biographical record—age, education, professional positions, public statements on educational issues, as well as the information obtained through reference checks—freshly in mind at the time of the interview.

The great merit of the interview is the impression it provides of personality, character, style. What kind of a person is this? How comprehensive is his or her understanding, how sharp is the mind, how quick the forensic skill? Has the candidate a sense of humor and a sense of compassion? Does the candidate become fresher and more impressive as the interview progresses, or does interest flag or repetition set in?

The interview also can throw some light on unresolved questions in the minds of committee members. The candidate's positions with regard to research, teaching, tenure, collective bargaining, graduate study, professional programs, and institutional governance can be explored. Ambiguous or contradictory comments from references about the candidate can be pursued and assessed.

Should candidates be asked a standard set of questions, or should each interview be custom-tailored? Each individual record will have its own blank spots or ambiguous areas that require clarification. This argues for tailoring the interviews to the individuals. The art of interviewing involves thinking about each interviewee in advance and designing the kind of questions that will exhibit the strengths and weaknesses, the professional competence, and the human qualities of the candidate.

However, all interviews should be alike in one important respect: They should each address the leadership qualities the committee agreed to seek. Even though the specific phrasing may vary from candidate to candidate (to reflect the committee's knowledge of the candidate's background), each aspect of the leadership qualities should be addressed to each candidate in distinct questions. Once these central questions have been asked, of all candidates, the committee can ask for elaboration or probe for additional information. Focus on the leadership qualities provides comparability among interviews and consistency in the committee's inquiries. Tailoring the questions to each candidate shows the candidate that the committee is well prepared and gives the candidate a sense that this is truly a personal interview.

To ensure that one questioner does not dominate the interview and that all of the leadership qualities are addressed, committee members can be assigned specific topics. The designated questioner need be responsible only for introducing the issue. Others then are free to follow up or to pursue the topic in greater breadth and detail.

# Tying Up the Results

Certain actions should immediately follow the interviews. First, committee members should record their individual impressions. Whether this is done on some previously agreed upon rating sheet or in the form of scribbled notes, reactions to the strengths and weaknesses of the candidates should be promptly recorded. With ten or so personalities being compared, it is easy to become forgetful or uncertain. The written record becomes invaluable.

At this point, the semifinalist list (candidates judged worth interviewing) should become even more select (candidates judged worth inviting to meet with board members or to visit the campus for wider exposure). How to handle candidates who survive the interviews and thus become finalists is the subject of the next chapter. The committee's decision about who are the survivors should follow on the heels of the last interview.

Once the decisions about finalists have been made, the chair or the committee's administrative officer on behalf of the chair should promptly contact all candidates and advise them of their status. If the committee's preliminary decision is still favorable, tell the candidate so—and use the occasion to make certain that the candidate is still actively interested. If the committee is not interested, the candidate should be so informed. If the committee must defer its decision pending completion of other interviews or the collection of more information, tell the candidate that he or she will be hearing from the committee within a specific amount of time. There is nothing so puzzling, and sometimes demoralizing, to the candidate as to be left dangling after the interview.

At this stage, the search for the new president is approaching its climax. Keeping in communication with finalist candidates is the most vital task for the committee and its chair.

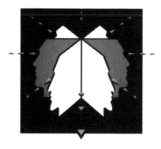

## CHAPTER SEVEN

# Finalist Candidates

After the interviews with semifinalist candidates, the real soul-searching begins. Occasionally, committee members will be unanimous in their preference, so convinced that they have identified just the right person to be the next president that they are prepared to make a recommendation to the trustees without further ado—without, that is, further checking into past performance and without further involvement of faculty, administrative staff, or students. Attractive as it may seem to bypass several steps in the laborious process of selection, this is a risky procedure. Sudden attraction is not always the best basis for a successful marriage.

Normally after interviews, the committee should be able to reduce its roster of candidates to five and preferably to three, depending on the number interviewed. At this point, most committees face two assignments. The first is to complete the investigation of the candidates (unless this already has been done), to obtain as much information as possible on their background and performance. The second is to expose them and the college or university community to one another to find out how compatible and enthusiastic they are after closer acquaintance and inspection. In a sense, the campus visit is one more step in checking out the candidate. Usually it is the last one.

## Rigorous Background Check

The normal procedure at this point is to complete the thorough investigation, started earlier, of the background and professional performance of potential candidates for campus visits. This investigation, the importance of which can hardly be overstated, can be conducted during the earlier screening process. But in view of the potential embarrassment resulting from local investigations, it is better to hold off until the list of candidates has been reduced to the finalists. Some candidates will strongly prefer that this kind of home-base investigation be deferred until after they have visited the campus that is seeking a president.

There comes a time, however, when local inquiries can no longer be postponed. They can and should be made with sensitivity and with the knowledge and permission of the candidates. If at this stage the candidate is still reluctant to have inquiries made on the home campus, the committee would be well advised to proceed with caution. The failure to investigate thoroughly can be a fatal mistake.

Presumably, during the screening process committees will have contacted the references supplied by the candidates. Although the candidate chose them, if the references have been carefully able to relate the individual's record to the leadership criteria, and if they have been astutely probed, their testimony has already provided a base of valuable information. Now it is important to fill out the picture.

The committee will want to be in touch with individuals who have worked closely with the candidate in his or her present and previous positions and who can give independent appraisals of the candidate's capacity to work with others, to delegate responsibility, to function under stress, and to exemplify in private as well as public life the qualities for which the committee is looking. This is the sort of assessment the committee needs at this stage. It should be a composite assessment, for no one sees the whole individual. Those for whom the candidate has worked may have a quite different picture from those who have worked for the candidate. Performance in one job may differ markedly from performance in another. The hostile critic needs to be discounted as much as the undiscriminating friend. Most strong candidates will have made *some* enemies.

Background information at this point can be obtained by telephone calls (it is too late for letters) and by personal visits to the candidate's campus. Telephone calls are less expensive and less time-consuming than on-site visits. Whether they are less satisfactory as well is debatable. Some people communicate better face-to-face. The visual and personal contact is likely to improve both the quality and the quantity of communication. People tend to speak more freely and fully than they write. Their inflections and hesitations can reveal information not to be found in a written statement.

Telephone inquiries at this stage, like the earlier preliminary calls, benefit from preparation, especially if calls are to be made by several individuals. The committee should design a series of remaining questions based upon the leadership criteria. As in interviews, the questions should not be recited mechanically; rather, they serve as a reminder to the caller of the range of information to be covered. Callers should feel free to explore, to ask for clarification of ambiguities, to request examples—in short, to carry on a conversation rather than an inquisition.

Before the call concludes, it is probably wise to probe for any information that could be damaging to the candidate. References will not ordinarily volunteer such information, but most will recognize its importance and will respond to an inquiry. To put the respondent at ease, the question might be approached indirectly; for example, "If I were to visit your campus and talk with some people who dislike the candidate, what reservations might I hear?" This will allow the respondent to answer objectively without feeling disloyal.

Callers will be well advised to write a brief summary following each call while the nuances are still fresh in mind. When all calls have been completed, the summaries can be shared with members of the screening committee, but under no circumstances should they go beyond that group. Even though the candidacy may already be public, respondents must be assured that their judgments will remain confidential.

# Visiting the Candidate's Campus: A Special Note

Although it is by no means the norm, it is increasingly common for an institution seeking a president to send an individual or a delegation to the home campuses of candidates. Sometimes the visits are scheduled before a subsequent visit of the candidate to the campus seeking the president. Just as often, the order of these visits is reversed.

In either case, there is no part of the search process that is more tricky and potentially harmful (nor as potentially beneficial) than visits to the candidates' campuses. The candidates must be informed and should themselves be given a chance to inform others of the impending visit. Surprising candidates at this point is almost a guaranteed way of losing them.

Planning the visit is essential. Committee members who wander aimlessly, questioning students and faculty at random, are likely to garner rumors and gossip in abundance but obtain little useful information. Rather, the committee should decide in advance with whom they wish to speak (probably in consultation with the candidate) and should schedule appointments (alternatively, the candidate may also schedule the visit). This will ensure that key contacts are available and have reserved sufficient time. The advice to committees on interviewing candidates applies equally to interviewing references; campus visitors should know what they want to ask and, to avoid overlooking anything, should assign to individuals the responsibility for pursuing specific lines of inquiry.

Taking notes of conversations is essential, especially since the visitors will bring back from the campus a kaleidoscope of impressions, many of them irrelevant to their investigation. A campus of shabby or unkempt appearance, for example, may create a negative impression for which the candidate cannot reasonably be held responsible if he or she has no authority over campus maintenance. Careful interview notes will keep the committee focused on relevant information.

It is rarely possible—or, indeed, desirable—for the full screening committee to visit each finalist's institution. Teams of two or three are more feasible and less costly. But if different members visit each campus, detailed planning becomes even more important to ensure the collection of comparable information. Here, again, an outside professional consultant can be very useful. With a broad background of information and trained in the technique of investigation, the professional knows what questions to ask, where the answers can be found, and how to evaluate conflicting responses.

Many search budgets cannot accommodate three or four on-site visits, especially when candidates are widely scattered. If the committee must choose between traveling to the candidates' campuses or bringing the finalists for visits to its own campus, the latter will prove a far better investment. Moreover, many calendars will not permit visits to other sites, especially when classes are in session. In such circumstances, a well-organized series of telephone inquiries is a fully satisfactory substitute or, in some people's experience, the more desirable method. A thorough telephone canvass will elicit the necessary information.

# The Candidate's Campus Visit—
# Pluses and Minuses

Having winnowed its original roster of candidates by screening based on credentials, interviews, and investigations of past performance, the committee must now decide which candidates should be invited for campus visits.

A few presidents have been offered—and have accepted—appointment without ever having visited an institution. Presumably, they already were sufficiently familiar with the local scene to make a visit unnecessary or so desperate to leave their current jobs that they were quite prepared to leap into the unknown (not a good omen).

Earl W. Porter, former secretary of the University of Illinois and secretary for the board of trustees, was involved in a survey of the selection process for presidents of large, complex state universities, both multicampus and statewide systems. He found widespread reluctance among the top officers of these institutions to emerge as a candidate on another campus. Says Porter: "As a group, they are likely to be familiar with most of the universities that approach them, will have visited them from time to time, may know some of the staff, and have a general idea of the resources and influences. In short, they are in the club and their questions are more subtle. If they need information, it will be to update what they already know, to sound out the present situation on the board of trustees, to know the circumstances under which the incumbent is leaving. If they wish, they can inquire about these and other matters indirectly and quietly. A final public visit, during which they may be recognized, may be risky and of minimal value."[1]

Most candidates, however, will want to have their own look at the inviting institution. Unless they already are familiar with it, they will want to see what the campus is like—buildings, grounds, and location. They may want to get some measure of the faculty's concern for educational issues, the composition and quality of the student body, the structure and competence of the administrative staff. They will want to talk with administrative officers with whom they would be working. They may want to speak with the outgoing president for an assessment of future prospects. What they find may produce a negative reaction; or, hesitant and skeptical before the visit, they may now find themselves attracted to the presidency.

At the same time, the various constituencies on campus will be eager to see what the candidates look like, what impression they make, whether they are educators or managers, scholars or fund-raisers. These constituencies would like to feel that they had some voice in the final selection. Faculty members will sometimes resent what they see as a deliberate indifference to their concerns and their judgment if they are not allowed a preview and may react with hostility to a new president they have never seen. And because it is important that the new president at least start with the goodwill of these constituencies, there are persuasive reasons to bring the final few to campus.

Yet there are clear and present dangers in public campus visits. The most obvious is that the candidate's cover will be blown. Because of this, the committee chair's phone call to each finalist must do more than congratulate the candidate. A diplomat's finesse is required. The chair must indicate that the search now becomes public; that the finalists will be invited to visit the institution; that a bulletin announcing the finalists will be issued to the campus, followed almost immediately by a news release to the press; and that the chair will prepare a brief biography—a page or two of narrative—for public distribution.

Rarely will a candidate object to exposure at this point, especially if it has been clear from the outset that such exposure would be required. Public announcement of finalists has become a common practice throughout higher education, and the candidate is more likely to be flattered than miffed. Some will ask for a short delay before the announcement so that colleagues and trustees can be informed before the news appears in the morning paper. Of course, candidates should be asked what additional information they would like before their visit and whom they will want to talk with when they arrive.

A second danger is that the appearance of several candidates on campus turns the selection into a pseudo-popularity contest. But an undesirable atmosphere can be contained by structuring a visit appropriately.

A third danger lies in the invitation to political maneuvering. Subtle (and sometimes not so subtle) campaigns can be carried on in favor of one candidate. Supporters of an inside candidate can leak their preferences to the press, with the result that outside candidates will feel insulted. Instructions from the committee to the community, establishing clearly that only individual reactions to individual candidates will be considered by the committee—no votes, petitions, or rallies—helps to focus the final stages on leadership issues rather than interest-group politics.

Finally, some candidates may take umbrage at the notion of putting on what is perceived to be a show for the benefit of faculty or students. The entire concept is offensive to them. They are prepared to be judged *in camera* by a selection committee or by the board as a whole where their merits or defects can be carefully weighed, but they are not interested in a public forum where their fate is decided by the mood of the audience. But if a visit is carefully organized and candidates are assured that the campus visit is but one of several ways by which they will be assessed, they should be able to see a visit as compatible with the dignity of the office to which they aspire.

We emphasize again that presidents, no matter how outstanding, must live with faculty, students, administrative officers, alumni, state education officials, and others. To be effective, they must have the support of powerful groups. The best way of ensuring the support of those groups at the start is by involving them in the selection. In practice, the best way of doing this is to have the key constituencies represented on the search and screening committees and to have those committees maintain rapport with their constituencies. This is not only a legitimate delegation of authority, it is an essential one.

Each search and screening committee will have to decide for itself how to manage the public announcement and campus visits. Where premature disclosure is not a problem, one important issue is removed. Where candidates are eager to meet with faculty and students, they should be accommodated. Traditional practices and the temper of the campus may suggest one procedure rather than another. Whatever the decision, plans need to be made with great care and shared in detail with both the candidates and the campus community. The committee cannot allow itself to forget that candidates still need to be courted.

# Introducing the Campus

One-day visits are barely adequate. A day and a half to two full days are much better. One state university arranged visits of four days each for its four finalists. Spouses should be included, since they obviously will influence the candidate's decisions. The campus should concentrate on one candidate at a time, not only to avoid the embarrassment of candidates bumping into one another but also to extract as much advantage as possible by focusing on one individual.

Decisions must be made about who will meet the candidate and under what circumstances. All interested faculty members or selected representatives of divergent faculty groups? Students at large or members of the student government association? Administrative officers, representatives of the denomination with which the institution is related (if any), local alumni, community leaders, state educational officers (if public), and trustees other than those on the selection committee also may figure into the mix. The candidate's wishes also must be considered, as must those of the spouse.

With so many people eager to get into the act, the candidate's schedule must be carefully planned well in advance. The board and committee chair of a church-related college in the South describe their program as follows: "When we brought a candidate to the community for an interview, we always requested that the candidate bring his or her spouse. We planned a very comprehensive schedule of interviews for these candidates, which included a meeting with all department heads on the faculty, a meeting with student leaders, a meeting with some trustees, and of course, meetings with members of the search committee. These meetings were normally culminated at the end of the second day with a dinner and social hour at my home, followed by a two- or three-hour session between the candidate and the members of the search committee."

The chair of the state university offers a general description of the four-day visits of the four candidates and their wives: "Their schedule was very busy, usually starting about 6:30 a.m. and concluding during the evening. We arranged several interviews and meetings with the major elements of the university, in addition to sessions with the selection committee. Actually, they met with over 100 members of the university. These included the board of trustees, top administrators, deans and department chairs, members of the faculty senate and representatives of the student body."

Exhibit N in the appendix presents a sample schedule for a campus visit.

Some screening committees find an initial meeting with the candidate a useful and gracious introduction to the campus. Other committees prefer to end the visit with such a meeting—to find out what kind of experience the candidate has had, what questions and reactions were generated, and what problems remain to be settled. If time and geography work out, the committee might do both.

All this sounds strenuous, and indeed it is—unavoidably so. One wants to be gracious, friendly, relaxed, to make a favorable impression on the candidate. Yet there is so much to be covered in a limited time. There is, however, a side benefit to setting up a fairly crowded schedule. That is the way the new president will be living his or her professional life, and it cannot hurt to observe the candidate under pressure.

Faculty and student members of the committee, or faculty and student advisory committees as the case may be, can take major responsibility for much of the candidate's visit. But each candidate should have one member of the committee or one administrative officer as host, whose responsibility it would be to shepherd the candidate from interview to interview, to introduce and to explain, to make special arrangements when necessary, to alter the schedule if desired, and to answer questions the candidate might have about specific meetings. The host should meet the candidate at the airport or wherever the candidate arrives, make certain that overnight accommodations are satisfactory and attractive, see that the candidate arrives at appointments on time, and in general stay with the candidate until departure.

At group meetings, the host may be present—to mediate if necessary, to observe reactions, and to interpret to the candidate afterwards why certain questions were raised and who pursued a certain line of inquiry. At individual conferences with administrative officers, the host's presence is normally not necessary and may interfere with candid communication.

Arrangements also should be tailored to the needs of the candidate's spouse. Prior to the campus visit, the spouse's interests should be ascertained and an independent agenda designed. Some of that agenda will overlap with that of the candidate. If the spouse has a career, he or she will want to know about employment opportunities, either off campus or in the university. The committee should familiarize itself with the institution's nepotism policies so it can convey accurately any restrictions on the spouse's employment by the institution.

If there are young children, both parents will be curious about child care and schooling. Since the candidate will be fully occupied in learning about the university, the spouse may wish to schedule an independent visit with school officials. If there is a president's house on campus, both will want to inspect it together, but if other housing arrangements are needed, the spouse may welcome a brief survey of local real estate. A husband or wife who runs marathons, plays string quartets, or competes at chess may want to know about local opportunities. Every effort should be made to plan a constructive schedule for the spouse.

# Educating the Candidates

The campus visit is an opportunity for the candidate to become acquainted with the institution and vice versa. Except for inside candidates, it is a vitally important opportunity. A sensible and realistic candidate will want to know as much as possible about the institution whose destiny may ultimately be his or her responsibility.

Each candidate invited to campus should receive a packet of information about the college or university that expands on that provided to candidates invited for interviews. At this stage, no important information can ethically be withheld. The institution's full financial picture, its admissions history and projections, financial-aid data, accreditation reports, and consultant's reviews all should be made available to candidates, not only to allow each to make a sound decision but also to begin building a relationship of trust. Exhibit M contains a list of useful materials.

The intelligent candidate will have studied this material in advance and will arrive with questions about finances, governance structure, temper of faculty and students, public relations, enrollment trends, collective bargaining (where it exists), and the like. Every finalist should be given full opportunity to learn the whole story.

A committee and board that cannot ensure candid and thoughtful responses to candidate questions likely will discourage a promising finalist or will be surprised down the road with an unhappy new president. Any serious problem areas should be openly discussed. It is good practice to provide opportunities for final candidates to meet privately with key officers and faculty members. Many sensitive questions can be explored during these meetings.

The campus visit also can be a unique opportunity to persuade the candidate of the worth of the institution—the quality of the educational program, the commitment of the faculty, the enthusiasm of the students, the conviction that all problems are surmountable and the future is exciting. All who will meet with the candidate need to be alerted to the importance of making the institution attractive. Sometimes they will naively assume that anyone would want to be president of "their" institution. Sometimes with the best of intentions, sometimes with the worst, and often without any thought at all, individuals can be very rough on candidates. That helps neither the candidate nor the institution.

# Anticipating the Appointment

Candidates will be concerned about the terms of their employment. One does not aspire to wealth by becoming a college or university president, but it would be naive to assume that candidates—even those in religious orders— are indifferent to financial considerations.

For the most part, candidates are understandably hesitant about making inquiries regarding their remuneration, for fear of seeming to put material considerations ahead of more important matters. Many are prepared to proceed on the formula stated by one president-elect: "A number of things were taken on faith—and that faith was justified." But candidates also might sympathize with the comment of one private college president: "As an inexperienced 'applicant' I regret that I treated terms of appointment rather casually in order not to appear 'pushy.' " A state university president five months after taking office wrote: "At no time have I received a formal job offer. Salary and fringe benefits were in doubt until the week I assumed office." Unfortunately, such situations are not unusual. But this is demeaning to the appointee and sets a poor tone for the new president.

The terms of employment need to be discussed long before the time of official appointment. The period of the campus interview is the most appropriate time. A subsequent visit to the campus or preliminary meeting with trustees is a possible but risky alternative. If the matter is postponed until time of appointment, the committee and the board risk the withdrawal of the chosen candidate, who may find the terms unacceptable. If they delay until a public announcement has been made, they are even more vulnerable.

Negotiation over salary and perquisites is not the proper function of the search and screening committee unless it consists entirely of trustees. Even then, the subject is better left to the committee or board chair. One or the other, should, by agreement, take the initiative in advising the candidates as to what the college or university is prepared to offer—not necessarily the precise terms, but certainly the range of total compensation. It also is important to ask the candidate whether the compensation package is acceptable—and to get an unequivocal answer in return. The negotiators must be sensitive to any special circumstances and be prepared to respond to them. For example, if the top finalist must sell his or her house, is the institution prepared or willing to consider financial incentives in the event it must be sold below market value?

# The Social Dimension

A college or university presidency, far more than most occupations, includes a variety of rituals and ceremonies among its requirements. These, it should be emphasized, are an aspect of the job, not a voluntary activity. As David Riesman notes, "If one doubts the importance of the ceremonial role, consider the position of the president of a leading sports power ... who fails to show up, along with the governor and the regents, at the big football game, whether with an out-of-state rival or the neighboring land-grant or flagship campus."[2]

Many of these ceremonies take the form of social events over which the president presides as host. Although the president has some control over the frequency and style of hospitality and considerable control over the scheduling, tradition demands an active social calendar. In the course of the year, the president is expected to extend gracious entertainment to trustees, faculty, donors, students, alumni, and perhaps legislators and visiting dignitaries.

When academic presidents were almost exclusively married men, the social responsibilities of the post were ordinarily managed by their wives who served as unpaid volunteers. However, the changing shape of American family life has affected college presidencies no less then other occupations. Presidents these days may be male or female, single or married, and, if married, may have spouses with independent careers of their own. Each of these patterns requires its own solution to the management of social obligations. Trustees need to be prepared to discuss their expectations with the visiting candidate (and spouse, if any) and what resources the institution offers to support the president's social role. (For an in-depth look at such matters, read *Public Roles, Private Lives,* an AGB Special Report by Roberta H. Ostar.[3])

If the candidate is single, for example, will the campus provide a housekeeper? A social assistant to draft guest lists, issue invitations, plan menus, and pay bills? Will the campus food service cater events at the president's house? Even if the house is off campus and privately owned? Will the president's house be available for use by on-campus groups? By off-campus groups? If so, who will schedule its use? Prepare for, monitor, and clean up after visitors? Many of the same questions will apply if the candidate is married to a working spouse, male or female. (A 1990 survey of presidential spouses showed 43 percent of female spouses employed either full-time or part-time, and 100 percent of male spouses employed full-time.[4])

When a candidate is married to a nonworking spouse, the spouse—still usually a wife—may prefer to assume the management of social responsibilities, whether as a volunteer or as a paid staff member. Trustees should be careful, however, not to assume that she will do so. Her preferences should be fully and candidly discussed. If she wishes to be salaried (surveys of spouses show that 20 percent to 40 percent prefer this option), some problematic issues arise. Will she, for example, be evaluated and if so, by whom? If not salaried, she may prefer another form of compensation, for example, a retirement plan or paid travel to professional meetings with her husband. Or she may welcome the opportunity to volunteer and thereby earn the satisfaction that comes from making an important contribution. Public recognition by the board of her voluntary services, something that currently is too infrequently bestowed, may count significantly as a substitute for other forms of compensation.

In any case, whether salaried or voluntary, she will need adequate support—staff, budget, and authority—to do her job well. Although specific details cannot be settled during a campus visit, the presidential couple can be assured that the board understands and intends to support the vital social dimension of the executive role.

# Aftermath of the Visit

At the end of the visit, or immediately thereafter while impressions are fresh, the reactions of people on campus need to be collected. These should be in written form and should be the judgments of individuals, not of groups. The committee might provide faculty and students with forms on which to summarize their reactions with respect to the leadership criteria. As previously mentioned, it is important that the campus constituents be clearly informed that only individual assessments of the candidates will be considered by the committee.

The end of the visit is also the time to find out whether the candidate is still actively interested. The candidate may be told that he or she is one of three or four whom the committee is prepared to recommend to the board, and that the committee needs to know whether the candidate will accept the position if offered, assuming that satisfactory terms can be negotiated.

Some candidates object to this procedure on the ground that the decision is too complex and too momentous to be made unless they are dealing with an actual offer. One can sympathize with the reaction. At the same time, it must be recognized that the offer of the presidency is a complex and momentous decision for the trustees. If an offer is made, word sometimes leaks out. If the offer is turned down, the resulting situation may be awkward. Other candidates, who under other circumstances would be happy to accept, may withdraw their names. Thus, to protect the reputation of the candidates as well as their own self-interest, trustees need to know in advance whether the candidate will accept the offer, assuming a mutually agreeable contract can be negotiated.

After the visits, with campus impressions as additional data, the committee must decide on its recommendations in accordance with its original charge from the board. With these recommendations, the committee completes its major assignment.

There remain for the committee certain chores that are discussed in the last two chapters. Candidates must be notified of the final decision. Announcements must be prepared. A record of the committee's work and an analysis of the number and nature of the candidates considered must be compiled and filed for future reference. Files must be stored in a secure location for one year in case official inquiries are subsequently made. Apart from these, the final step belongs to the board, which must make the appointment and set the terms and conditions.

---

[1] "The Presidential Search as the Presidents See It," *AGB Reports* (vol. 25, no. 1, January/February 1983), p. 46. Also see Porter, "Presidential Selection at Large State Universities," *AGB Reports* (vol. 24, no. 6, November/December 1982).

[2] "The President's Spouse," in *The Partnership Model*, ed. Roberta H. Ostar (Washington, D.C.: AASCU 1986), p. 4.

[3] Roberta H. Ostar, *Public Roles, Private Lives* (Washington, D.C.: Association of Governing Boards of Universities and Colleges).

[4] Ibid.

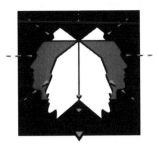

## CHAPTER EIGHT

# Appointing the President

The final decision, now before the board of trustees, it not always as easy as it might seem. Should search committees conclude with a single recommendation, or should they present to the board of trustees a slate of acceptable candidates? And if the latter, should they rank them in order of preference or, as the trustees of one private university of national stature required, present them in alphabetical order? The answer lies in the initial charge from the trustees, and this is just one of the many reasons that charge needs to be stated in unequivocal terms.

The screening committee, on instructions from the board, may have recommended only one candidate. If the committee includes several board members, especially board leaders, and if the board can be swayed by those members, a single choice may be acceptable to the board. A much more difficult situation develops if a committee that lacks such board strength recommends a single candidate. In either case, the board must either ratify or reject the committee's decision. If the board chooses rejection, it may ask the committee for another recommendation, or it may replace the committee—with understandable feelings of resentment on the part of the original members. Naturally, considerable time is lost.

Such regrettable events could have been avoided if the board's original charge had stipulated two—or better yet, three—recommended candidates. When the committee recommends more than one candidate, the board can then make its choice either on the basis of the committee's data and rating or after conducting its own interviews with the candidates.

It is worth noting, however, that quite a few committee chairs have reported that, in spite of a mandate to recommend more than one candidate, they had ended up with only one nomination and were able to persuade the trustees to accept their decision. Conversely, one committee with instructions to present a single name was unable to decide between two candidates and recommended both to the board. The board then made its own choice.

The arguments for a single nomination are obviously quite strong. A conscientious committee, by the end of its labors, will know more about the candidates and their "fit" with the institution than trustees who have not been directly involved. This position is strongly argued by the committee chair of a well-known church-related college: "When the committee is constituted as ours was to represent trustees (including alumni trustees), faculty, and students—I personally feel that it would be an avoidance of responsibility to recommend several candidates simultaneously. There is no possible way by which other trustees, alumni, faculty, and students could make the same type of careful and prayerful appraisal of the crop of candidates or even three or four of them, as was done by the committee. Any thoughtful committee would be unlikely to find several of equal merit."

Furthermore, a single nomination flatters the nominee. He or she can better endure the break in confidentiality that may occur at this final stage, since the chances of appointment are high. The risks of turning the selection into a popularity contest are reduced. If the candidate is at all reluctant or undecided, the awareness that he or she is the committee's one choice may be the decisive turning point.

Finally, there is the virtue based on necessity: The committee may have no real choice. The record suggests that committees seeking a slate of candidates frequently end up with only one on whom the members can all agree and whom they are prepared to recommend.

On the other hand, a single nomination, in spite of the legal authority of the board to decline to appoint, puts the all-important decision in the hands of the search and screening committee. In effect, it usurps the legitimate prerogative of the board. If the trustees or regents are genuinely to exercise the power of appointment, they should have a choice. This is clearly desirable where the committee is composed of nontrustees or where the trustee members play a very minor role. It may become less important where the committee is dominated by its trustee members, where it has the full confidence of the board, and where the latter has been kept fully informed of the committee's progress.

It is sometimes suggested that the mark of a well-conducted search is its success in finding three or more candidates, all of whom would make, in the eyes of the committee, outstanding presidents. Such an outcome is certainly ideal and safer, because candidates have a way of withdrawing at the last moment. Occasionally, the leading candidate will find the terms of the offer unsatisfactory or will accept an offer from another institution. In such situations, it saves time and, more important, embarrassment if the board can turn at once to another choice (who, if strong enough, is actually an alternative first choice) rather than ask the committee to return to the process of screening and recommending.

The choice between a single recommendation and several will vary from institution to institution. It will depend for some on legislative or bylaw regulations. For others, the temper of the institution will determine the choice. Where the number of candidates is severely limited (as in some church-related institutions), a single recommendation may be a matter of necessity. A high degree of mutual trust among the various constituencies, general agreement on the kind of person wanted and needed, and the absence of divisive forces politicizing the campus are conducive to allowing the search committee to conduct its work unfettered. Where these conditions do not exist, it is better for the trustees to have a choice of candidates and to be recognized as making the decision.

It is presumably this emphasis on the role of the trustees that leads some boards to request an unranked slate of names, but there are other reasons to do so as well. If the board, for reasons that must remain private, cannot come to terms with the top-ranked candidate, it may be accused, however unjustly, of ignoring the committee's recommendation. This can only lead to bad feelings. Moreover, no president should take office knowing or subsequently learning that he or she was the committee's second choice—for obvious reasons!

The board will certainly wish to avail itself of the committee's extensive knowledge of each candidate, but it need not rely on rankings to do so. It can request the committee to prepare a summary of each candidate's strengths and limitations or a statement of the reasons for their support of each, or it can ask the committee chair to describe the pros and cons of each candidate in the committee's estimation. These methods give the trustees the benefit of the committee's wisdom while avoiding the disadvantages of ranking the candidates.

# The Board Appointment

Presidents are appointed by boards, and therefore the final act in the search process is the official board decision. It is a decision that should be made by the full board.

The board may wish to conduct its own interviews with one or more finalists, particularly if few trustees have had an opportunity to meet the candidates. Or the board may have such confidence in the search and screening committee(s) that the board is willing to act on the recommendations alone. In making the appointment, the board should confirm the terms negotiated or vote authority to the chair or a special board committee to settle the terms of employment. Giving the chair such authority is clearly preferable.

# Terms of Appointment

"Terms of appointment" is a broad concept comprising a wide variety of conditions and circumstances. Unfortunately, boards and presidents often give less thought to these matters than to the business of selection. Agreement is frequently postponed until circumstances force a decision.

In the majority of situations, goodwill and common sense prevail, but there is disturbing evidence that newly elected presidents have become disappointed or disillusioned by unfulfilled expectations or, worse, broken promises. A lot of heartache, disaffection, and future trouble would be avoided if boards, and chancellors in statewide systems, were clearer and more specific at the time of appointment on the practical and professional arrangements for the new president. These fall into three categories: financial, professional, and administrative.

# Financial

The financial offer should cover most (though not necessarily all) of the following items:

salary

annuity or pension provisions

medical or health insurance

life insurance

moving expenses

president's house plus

> maintenance and repairs
> *or* housing allowance

household help

entertainment expenses

automobile and expenses

travel expenses

Some of these items need little comment. Provision for retirement income, whether through TIAA-CREF or a state employee pension plan or some institutionally funded plan, is standard. Many medical or health insurance programs include some provision for life insurance. It is customary to provide moving expenses for the new president and his or her family.

Since the president's job requires extensive travel, these costs should be reimbursed. If the candidate is married, perceptive boards will encourage the wife or husband to travel with the president by covering the spouse's travel costs as well (state law permitting, in the case of tax-supported institutions). These arrangements, however, should be spelled out in a separate agreement with the spouse.

An official automobile is an optional item. It is fairly common for public institutions to make one available. So do many larger and better financed private colleges and universities, often through cooperative arrangements with a local car dealer.

Housing provisions for the president and his or her family vary. Some institutions—for example, the majority of community colleges and some of the smaller private and church-related colleges—make no provisions, on the assumption that the president's salary is sufficient to provide for this and other family expenses. In periods of inflation, presidents may prefer to own their own houses in order to develop equity against the time when they will have to fend for themselves.

The majority of institutions, however, do provide a president's house or a housing allowance as part of the compensation package and because they expect the president to carry on a certain amount of official entertaining at home. This is often a larger and more expensive establishment than the individual otherwise would choose. When the house belongs to the college or university, it should be understood that repairs and normal maintenance are the responsibility of the institution. This may apply as well to domestic service and to the not-inconsiderable costs of official entertaining. If the residence is to be enlarged or renovated, this should be stipulated and a cost range established. There should be clear understanding from the start about who pays for what. In some cases, when the official residence may not be suitable, other arrangements will need to be made—and agreed upon in advance.

A word of caution, however, is in order. The press and the public may misunderstand the function of the president's house. Indeed, they may fail entirely to recognize that social activity is an obligatory part of the president's professional role. Yet a 1991 survey showed that presidents, on average, hosted well over 60 events a year in their homes. In the mid-Atlantic region, the average topped 80 events, with an annual average of more than 4,000 guests.[1]

When the president's house is perceived as a private residence rather than what it actually is—a specialized campus facility similar to a reception hall or dining commons—difficulties may result. Costly renovations or improvements to the residence have been known to trigger heated press criticism and public outcry. Often these objections have been directed at the president as an individual, and presidents of tax-supported institutions have been especially vulnerable targets.

Trustees should make every effort to avoid such needless contention. Before the new president arrives, the board, on its own initiative, should ensure that the house contains the amenities needed for official entertaining and that its condition is excellent throughout. If public criticism ensues, the board should explain its intentions and take full responsibility. The president should not be allowed to become the victim of public misunderstanding.

# Professional

Academic administration is a professional job. With the exception of a few individuals drawn from business, the military, law, or the ministry, college and university presidents are pursuing a professional career in education—a career that usually begins with teaching and progresses through various educational and administrative steps to the presidency. Continued professional growth is extremely important not only to the president's effectiveness in his or her present assignment but also in anticipation of a post-presidential career. Boards of trustees can make provision for this need by means of adequate vacation, leaves of absence, extramural activities, academic appointment (with or without tenure), and cultivation of professional competence.

Provision for a formal vacation period should be part of the contract or letter of appointment. One month is normal, but sometimes six weeks or two months are agreed upon, especially where the president uses some of the "vacation" time for writing annual reports or making studies that cannot be efficiently pursued in the midst of campus pressures. Board chairs need to keep a friendly eye on the emotional condition of their presidents and should encourage them to take occasional breaks from the demands of their office. Business executives restore their energy and drive and gain perspective on broad issues by taking winter as well as summer holidays; college and university presidents need similar periodic opportunities for recuperation and rejuvenation. In the long run, the institution gains.

In 1971, the Association of American Colleges adopted a statement on administrative leaves of absence which reads in part: "Because of the unique position of the president and the special planning required for implementation of a presidential leave, the governing board of the institution should assume responsibility for initiating this leave program and provide special funding to support it." The resolution emphasizes that the president should not be required to apply for a leave as though it were a special favor. It concludes: "As for any administrative leave, the precise terms of a presidential leave should be agreed to and stated in writing in advance."

Presidential leaves are less uncommon today than in the past. Their value is being more widely recognized. Trustees are becoming more concerned about receiving the maximum return on their human investment. "Given the substantial investment a governing board makes in finding a president," writes Joseph Kauffman, "it is simply good management for the board to conserve this important resource. Leadership is a scarce and precious asset that should not be taken for granted."[2]

Some presidents will wish to teach, and others will seek recognition of their scholarly attainments and academic leadership. Both of these interests can be addressed by a professorial appointment in one of the academic divisions of the institution. If the appointment is a tenured one, the president is cushioned in case of a fall from grace or in the event he or she chooses to retire early from the presidency. The board will want to review its standing policies on the award of tenure and get faculty agreement, especially in public institutions, before negotiating with the candidate.

Just as some college and university presidents continue to teach—a practice that, however desirable and laudable, is becoming increasingly difficult to manage—so others will continue active participation in professional societies and conferences. In due course, others will be invited to serve on corporate and foundation boards. Federal, state, and local agencies may request service on special public-service commissions or panels.

All these serve to keep professional interests alive and enlarging. They add new dimensions to the president's stature, new perspectives to his or her understanding of contemporary society, and positive publicity for the institution. Active participation in religious organizations is not only an extramural outlet for the individual, but may also be an important contribution to the institution—especially for the president of a church-related college. Presidents, who have little leisure for reflection, should seize opportunities for off-campus activities that will give them perspective on their jobs. The need for this cannot be written into a contract, but its value should be recognized by the board.

Staying alive professionally also is an important hedge against the day when the president may want other employment or when the board may perceive the need for a change of leadership. The president may, of course, move on to another college or university appointment, but he or she may well return to former scholarly work or to a related field. The more professionally competent the president is, the greater the likelihood of a successful transition.

# Administrative

Administrative arrangements should include some or all of the following:

starting date

retirement date

length of appointment

conditions of termination

criteria for performance

provision for review and evaluation

The starting date for a new president normally presents no difficulty, though it may need to be negotiated if the college or university is facing a sudden crisis or if the president-elect has commitments that cannot be gracefully altered.

Unless the institution's bylaws or a board resolution specify the age of retirement for administrative officers as well as faculty, the appropriate date of retirement for the incoming president (on the assumption, of course, that all will go well) should be discussed, and the proper time for settling this matter is prior to or at the time of appointment.

It should be clearly understood that all presidential appointments are at the pleasure of the board, for once the trustees have lost confidence in the president, the good of the institution requires his or her departure. Should presidential appointments be formally renewed year by year? Should they be for an indefinite period? Should they run for a given term of, say, five years?

In recent years, there has been a distinct trend toward term appointments. Clark Kerr, former president of the University of California and former chairman of the Carnegie Council on Policy Studies on Higher Education, recommends that the president be given "a term appointment of reasonable length. This will give him, except under exceptional circumstances, a fixed period on which he can plan. At the end of the term, he will have an easy opportunity to review his own desires and for others to review his conduct. If he is reappointed, he will have received a reaffirmation of his authority as he meets new crises. In any event, opponents will not feel that they must wait forever for a change unless they mount massive opposition. A term of office could relax their opposition."[3]

Whether a board appoints the president for a given term, which may of course be renewed, or for an indefinite period, it must realistically assume that the president is not likely to remain forever. It would be reassuring to have the president continue for ten to fifteen years, but ten or fewer years is the likely prospect. Whether the departure occurs in accordance with some agreed-upon schedule or as the result of board dissatisfaction with the president's performance, or the president's dissatisfaction with the board's performance, plans for the separation need to be laid in advance.

Boards and candidates assume, as do people getting married, that their lives together will be harmonious. They look to the future with confidence. It seems, therefore, slightly indecent to want to discuss what they should do if they find that they cannot live and work together. Yet this is precisely what is needed. The board needs to know, after a period of initial acceptance has passed, that the new president will not desert on short notice, and the president needs assurance that he or she will be given reasonable leave with salary if circumstances require a change. Further, the absence of clear termination arrangements after a presidential tenure has reached a reasonable length can lead to lawsuits, which are expensive and damaging to the institution.

The sensible board will set forth the terms, conditions, and circumstances of separation at the end of a first period of service—usually three to five years. A separation provision may not be necessary during the first contract or term of service. Indeed, including it then, except under unusual circumstances, could convey a number of undesirable messages. But such a provision should at least be included in all subsequent renewals.

# Form of Agreement

What form should the agreement between the board and the new president take? With the exception of only one group, the most widely used form is a letter from the board chair (or the chief executive officer in a statewide system) to the candidate setting forth the terms and conditions. The one exception consists of community colleges, where formal contracts are the rule. But the use of contracts also is on the upswing in four-year institutions.

What is really surprising is the number of institutions where the agreement is entirely oral. One might expect to find this occasionally in private institutions, but it occurs in a small percentage of public ones as well. A formal written statement covering the terms of the appointment ought to be made in every instance. The difference between a contract and a contractual letter is a fine one, but the difference between a written and an oral agreement is the difference between a good operation and a sloppy one. There is no standard contract or contractual letter covering the many items just discussed, but the foregoing checklist should be sufficient in drawing up a satisfactory statement of agreement.

# The President's Spouse

When the appointee is a married man whose wife will undertake some services for the institution, her services should be engaged independently. A separate agreement should be drafted, outlining her responsibilities and compensation, if any. It should specify whatever stipend or other benefits have been agreed to: retirement plan, insurance, travel expenses, staff support, and so forth. Some institutions have considered a spousal annuity such as the one offered by TIAA-CREF. Like her husband, a female spouse should not be expected to operate under an oral agreement with its attendant uncertainties. Occasionally, a male spouse enjoys the role of host for the institution. In such cases, similar agreements should be considered.

# Criteria for Selection and Performance Review

To repeat what is obvious, but too frequently ignored: The president is the agent of the board of trustees or regents. The board sets the policies—very often at the president's instigation and always, one hopes, with the president's participation. The president must operate within such policies, and it is the board's responsibility to judge whether the president operates well or poorly. How can the president know what is expected, and how can the trustees judge how well the president has lived up to expectations unless there is prior agreement on what the institution needs?

Here the leadership criteria that served as the basis of selection throughout the search once again come into play. These criteria reflect the board's agreement—and often that of the entire university—on the tasks most urgently facing the institution. Incorporated into the appointment letter—and approximately translated into a more action-oriented set of tasks, the original expectations serve to remind the appointee what his or her priorities must be and at the same time provide the board with fair and appropriate criteria for assessment. The standard of performance for evaluating the president is the attainment of these priorities or appropriate movement toward that end. Far too often a president is evaluated in a crisis on criteria not explicitly discussed at the time of appointment, frequently by board members who were not on the board at the time of selection.

Although the president is constantly being judged, the close of the academic year is a useful time to take stock. An annual appraisal often is kept deliberately informal. The president may be expected to review the year's achievements, and the board may respond orally or in writing. Many boards add a welcome grace note in expressing their appreciation of the president's efforts. The annual review is often linked to adjustments in presidential compensation.

A more formal evaluation at the end of the fourth or fifth year is becoming increasingly common. This may involve other campus constituencies in addition to the trustees and may utilize the services of an objective external consultant. If such a procedure is contemplated, it should be specified in the letter of appointment or agreed upon within the first two years of a president's service. Suggested ways to conduct both formal and informal evaluations appear in *Presidential Assessment,* a companion volume published by AGB.[4]

# Announcing the Appointment

The choice has been made, the terms agreed upon, and the appointment made official. There remains the public announcement, which is an institutional responsibility, and the private notification to unsuccessful candidates, which is the committee's task. Both have been anticipated in the communications plan drafted at the outset of the search. The two aspects now need to be coordinated.

Excitement will be high and rumors rampant. There is every reason for making a public announcement at the earliest possible date and with agreement on precise timing by both parties. That date must of course allow the president-elect time to notify colleagues and superiors before they read about the appointment in the newspapers.

It must also allow time for the selection committee to notify any finalists who have not already bowed out of the picture. (Sadly, this necessary courtesy is forgotten all too often.) If only a few remain, telephone calls will be the most gracious way to inform them of the choice. No one who has any reason to believe he or she might still be in the running should learn of the decision by newspaper or radio, as has been the case in more instances than one would like to believe. Not only is prior notification the only professional and decent thing to do, but it also prevents a well-recognized finalist from conveying to others a bad image of the institution.

As a courtesy to those most directly affected, faculty, student, and administrative staff leaders should be informed before the public announcement.

News releases will need to be prepared and distributed at the proper time. Copies might be sent to all candidates and to those who have nominated candidates—with appropriate cover letters thanking them for their interest and help. A little extra effort at this point will enhance the reputation and standing of the institution.

Alumni will need to be informed either by special announcement from the committee or the board chair or by an article in the alumni magazine reviewing the search, selection, and appointment. An example of a typical announcement is appended as Exhibit O.

---

[1] Roberta H. Ostar, *Public Roles, Private Lives,* (Washington, D.C.: Association of Governing Boards of Universities and Colleges 1991), pp. 18–19.

[2] *The Selection of College and University Presidents,* (Washington, D.C.: Association of American Colleges 1974), p. 61.

[3] "Presidential Discontent" in *Perspectives on Campus Tensions,* (Washington, D.C.: American Council on Education 1970), pp. 159–60.

[4] John B. Nason, *Presidential Assessment,* (Washington, D.C.: Association of Governing Boards of Universities and Colleges 1984), pp. 9–14.

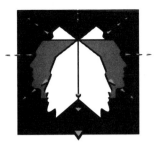

CHAPTER NINE

# Winding Down and Gearing Up

Before the excitement has quite subsided and the dust completely settled, a few final steps remain.

## Preserving the Record

For the guidance of future committees a final and comprehensive report of the entire process should be drafted and filed. Sometimes the committee chair assumes this responsibility; more often it is done by the committee's secretary or an administrative staff member.

The search for and selection of the new president is a defining event in the life of a college or university. Some future historian of the institution will welcome the light that a summary report will shed on a long-past event. But it will also serve a purpose in the nearer future. Memories quickly grow dim and erratic. Papers are lost or mislaid. The confidential documents regarding candidates must be filed under lock and key for one year in case any official or legal inquiries about the process arise.

The committee obviously hopes it will not have to undertake another search for a long time to come. Chances are, when another search does occur, the committee will consist of entirely different people. A detailed report on procedures, problems, and conclusions—which might well contain a section on what not to do—will be invaluable to a future committee.

One unusually well-organized committee appended the following list of documents to a three-page summary of its composition, mode of operation, and conclusions:

1. Flow chart (indicating process of finding and selecting candidates).
2. Charge to committee.
3. Membership of committee and how chosen.
4. Statement of leadership qualities.
5. Recruiting and communication plans.
6. Job description.
7. Advertisement(s).
8. Memo on affirmative-action plan.
9. Mailing lists.
10. Methods used for processing information.
11. List of questions for telephone interviews (for candidates reaching final stage).
12. Summary statistical report.

For institutions holding federal contracts, Executive Order 11246 requires that data pertaining to equal opportunity be preserved. In a 1975 memorandum explaining federal requirements, the director of the Office for Civil Rights wrote: "The Executive Order establishes the principle that federal contractors, including colleges and universities, are required to collect and maintain data on the race, sex, and ethnic identity of all applicants for employment. The collection and analysis of such data is recognized as an essential means of providing both the institution and the federal government with the information necessary to monitor the compliance posture of the institution."[1]

# Easing the Transition

Although the committee's work is now done, the board should prepare to help the new president make a good start.

Unless the president-elect is an insider, there will be problems of transition from the previous administration to new leadership. The president will have much to learn about new responsibilities. Because the outgoing president normally will leave maximum flexibility for the successor by making as few long-term decisions as possible, the incoming president will be faced with more than the normal run of important decisions.

Where the transition is a friendly one, the outgoing president can be expected to counsel the successor on critical issues, booby traps, and the like. A memorandum from the departing president might suggest various steps that would be of help to the new president and an advantage to the college.

It is extremely important that the new president start off well, for the first decisions and the first speeches to faculty, staff, and students will be examined very carefully and to a large extent will determine campus opinion. A transition team or committee might be appointed to serve for the first six months of the new president's tenure. This group might include some of the faculty members on the search and selection committee. If a committee is not advisable, a senior and respected member of the faculty might be asked to serve as special counselor to the president, to be called on for advice and inside information whenever needed. However, care should be taken that any transitional mechanism does not usurp the functions or prerogatives of established faculty governance.

One of the most difficult problems for new presidents, according to the findings of the Commission on Strengthening Presidential Leadership, is the number of "untouchables" or sacred cows on the administrative staff. The incoming president, if wise, will diligently try to work with the administrative team he or she inherits, but established administrative officers do not always accept new ideas or new leadership. New presidents are entitled to form their own management teams in due course and should be free to make changes designed to improve administrative effectiveness. Change becomes not only difficult but for all practical purposes impossible unless the board is prepared to support the president's judgment on who should stay and who should go. Where trustees have established friendships or close working relationships with administrators of long tenure, this issue can become especially delicate.

The president-elect may not have extensive administrative experience and may be lacking in certain technical tools of the trade. Sometimes the president-elect will take the initiative by proposing to take one or more management training courses, but often the board chair will need to encourage the new president to attend special institutes or to engage consultants in areas where the president needs support. Attendance at such an institute might even be part of the original agreement where both the committee or board chair and the new president agree that such skills need to be acquired.

# Conclusion

The analysis and recommendations contained in this study of presidential selection have emphasized continually the importance of the selection process in the life of the institution. For everyone concerned, the choice of a new president has important implications.

The analysis of institutional needs on which the criteria for the new president are based can unite trustees, faculty, administration, students, alumni, and state educational officers on the mission of the college or university. The long and intense work of trustees, faculty, students, and others on the search and screening committees breeds mutual understanding, and understanding breeds trust.

Many board chairs have testified to the healing and harmonizing effects of close cooperation in a common cause. Further, the manner in which the committee communicates with the many interested constituencies—the press, candidates, nominators, and references as well as students, faculty, staff, alumni, parents, and the local community—says something important about the nature and style of the institution. What can seem to be byproducts of the selection process can turn out to be among its most valuable—or damaging—results.

The purpose of this book has been to examine various ways in which college and university presidents have been selected and to extract certain guidelines, policies, and procedures that have proven effective. These will vary in detail from one type of institution to another, but the broad principles of what constitutes good practice remain the same for all. The analysis and recommendations here are intended to facilitate and improve the process, thereby strengthening colleges and universities at a critical point in their lives.

---

[1] David J. Hanson and Cyrena N. Pondrum, *Guide to Federal Regulations,* (Washington, D.C.: National Association of College and University Business Officers 1978)

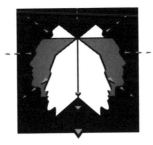

# Presidential Search

## EXHIBITS

# Exhibit A

## Sample: Board's Charge to Screening Committee

The Presidential Screening Committee, appointed to advise the Board of Trustees of _____ University, is composed of _____ board members, _____ faculty members, (optional: students, alumni, community representatives). The Committee's chair and spokesperson is Trustee _____

The Presidential Screening Committee is charged with recommending to the Trustees, not later than (date) an unranked list of three to five individuals who, in the Committee's judgment, are well qualified to lead _____ University as its next president. The Screening Committee is asked to base its recommendations upon the leadership criteria adopted by the Board of Trustees, as well as upon the Trustees' established policies with respect to equal opportunity and affirmative action.

The Board asks the Presidential Screening Committee, in discharging its duties, to conduct the following activities:

- Draft and place advertisements for the position, using the statement of leadership qualities as the basis for advertising;
- Actively solicit nominations and applications from a diverse group of well-qualified persons, including women and minorities;
- Oversee the receipt of and responses to applications and nominations from all sources;
- Screen applications using the leadership criteria as the basis for choice;
- Select and interview semifinalist candidates;
- Assist in checking references of semifinalists;
- Assist in arranging campus visits for finalist candidates and spouses;
- Report to the Board a summary of campus and community reactions to finalist candidates;
- Ensure that appropriate information about the University and the presidency is provided to candidates at each stage of the screening process;
- Ensure that confidentiality is strictly observed with respect to applicants and to the Committee's internal deliberations.

The Board of Trustees extends its gratitude to the members of the Presidential Screening Committee for accepting this demanding assignment. You have the Trustees' warmest wishes for a successful conclusion. Upon your wisdom the future of the University rests.

# Exhibit B

## Institutional Analysis: Issues to Consider

*Changes in Mission or Purposes.* Is the college or university at a point in its history where it either wants or needs to change its direction—that is, its goals and purposes? Community colleges do adjust to changes in the social-political-industrial character of their environment. State normal schools seek full-spectrum university status. Many church-founded colleges have evolved at some point into independent institutions. The importance of graduate education or research may change over the years.

*Fiscal Management.* In an era of limited if not actually declining resources, is the institution fiscally strong, weak, or somewhere in between? Is the business office well equipped to cope, or must the new president be prepared to shore up financial control?

*Resource Acquisition.* Is the institution adequately funded? Are new efforts required to increase public funding? Funding from private sources? From foundations? What special experience or skills should a new president possess within these areas? What skills can be learned and what role will the board play in educating the new president?

*Educational Expansion.* Is the institution under pressure to expand into new areas, and do faculty and trustees believe that such expansion would be desirable? Community colleges are almost always under pressure by sectors in the community to add vocational courses. Liberal arts colleges receive student pressure for more business courses and overseas programs. A university may have just made the decision to divest its dental or medical school, and another may have added an international track to its management program.

*Consolidation of Educational Programs.* Has proliferation over the years of courses, departments, schools, centers, and institutes weakened the capacity to survive? What many institutions need is not to expand, but to contract creatively. The president who can lead the institution into new areas and programs often has a different temperament and different attributes from the president who can manage retrenchment and consolidation.

*Enrollment.* What are the institution's enrollment prospects? Should an aggressive recruitment program be launched? Are there new sources of students? What changes in age, sex, and background of the student body are likely? What changes are desirable?

*Educational Quality.* Is it high, so that the only issue is to keep it that way? Is it good and, therefore, not a major focus of effort? Is it less than it ought to be? If so, is the problem primarily one of the quality of the faculty or of the values that permeate the institution? If improving the quality of the faculty is the central problem, the new president should have certain intellectual and personal qualities that will fit him or her for the kind of leadership required.

*Physical Plant.* Are the library, laboratories, classrooms, dormitories, athletic facilities, and social centers adequate for the desired size and character of the institution? Must a major effort be made to add new buildings or to renovate buildings that have been allowed to deteriorate? Some individuals find creative pleasure in building new buildings and in improving old ones. Others have interests focused on quite different ends.

*Collective Bargaining.* What will be the new president's attitude toward collective bargaining? Although faculty unions are more common in public than in private institutions, they are a reality that may require certain competencies or skills in the new president. How effective will he or she be in dealing with the union if one exists on campus? If one is being considered, will the new president try to stave it off or welcome it? The board's and faculty's own attitudes toward this issue are likely to incline them toward one candidate rather than another.

*Student Life and Activities.* How adequate are the institution's student life activities? These will vary enormously from nonresidential commuter colleges to private or church-related colleges where virtually all the students reside in dormitories. But every educational institution provides some extracurricular programs ranging from counseling to sports to social activities. Does the athletic program need to be reviewed? Have there been racial or ethnic tensions? Issues related to student life may require more attention than they have received.

*Governance.* Does it work well? Do the various constituencies have a voice in it, and are they satisfied? Is there pressure for change? Should the new president be expected to lead a reorganization of the governing structure?

*Self-Image.* How does the institution see itself? Is it satisfied with its image? This is a subtle matter of morale and institutional spirit.

## Public Four-Year Colleges and Graduate Universities

Public institutions face problems that private colleges and universities do not, and vice versa. In making a quick survey of where the institution stands and what its goals and needs will be over the next decade, public trustees and committee members will want to examine the following:

*External relations.* What is the status of the institution with respect to the central office of the statewide system, the governor, the education commissioner, and the legislature? Do communications need to be improved? Do external relations need major attention for the college or university to hold its own or improve its position?

*Regional economy.* Is the state's population growing or declining? In what ways is the economy likely to change? What new demands or pressures will the university experience?

*Multicampus issues.* How do local educational units relate to the central system office? Are changes likely to occur in this relationship? Will new units be added or existing ones closed? What political forces will affect decisions?

*Autonomy.* In what areas and to what extent can the trustees and administration make their own decisions regarding programs, plant, salary levels, and the like? How much political interference does the university suffer? Is the situation healthy, or is a major battle looming over the autonomy of the institution?

*Consolidation of control.* Is the university a reasonably unified whole, as the term "university" implies it should be? While consolidation of programs is an issue for all types of institutions, central control over the often semi-independent fiefdoms of the academic world often is a special problem for large state universities with extensive programs and services.

*Equal opportunity.* Are women and minorities well represented in faculty and staff? Many state institutions are struggling with the issues of equal opportunity and affirmative action, both in hiring—especially faculty—and in recruitment of students. Is the institution enrolling its share of able minority students? Has the institution moved to open admissions? If not, will it do so in the near future, and what adjustments will that require?

*Athletics.* Does the university have a sensible and defensible athletic program? Is there public and alumni pressure for bigger and better football or basketball teams? Do these sports play a disproportionate role in the institution's life and budget? Is the director of athletics largely independent, controlling funds and programs over which the administration has no voice?

# Private Colleges and Universities

*Sense of mission.* Although important for all types of institutions, this is particularly critical for the private college. Is the campus harmonious? Do faculty and administration and trustees work well together? Or is there antagonism and political infighting? Have recent issues exacerbated the situation? Must the new president provide charismatic leadership? Does the institution need someone who can help the board become more effective and involved?

*Student recruitment.* Does the institution face difficulties in maintaining a satisfactory number of applicants? How will conditions over the next decade affect student recruitment? What steps will need to be taken? Is the problem one of better public relations or better organization of the admissions office and procedures? What does this say about the kind of person who should be president?

*Quality of faculty.* What is and what should be the student-faculty ratio? While the improvement of educational quality is a question for the trustees of all institutions, the size and quality of the faculty is frequently an urgent problem for the private college. Is the faculty too large or too small? Does it need upgrading? What steps might be taken?

*New clientele.* Can and should the college or university compensate for the dwindling pool of 17- to 21-year-old students by recruiting older people? What changes in programs would this involve?

*Public relations.* How is the institution viewed in the surrounding community by alumni, donors, and friends? Does the institutional image need improvement? Do alienated alumni and friends need to be wooed back? Are there new publics the college should seek to interest?

*Church relations.* For church-related colleges, are there problems with the founding and/or sponsoring denominations? Is the problem one of rekindling church or denominational interest and support? Or is it one of reducing the influence and control of the denomination that supports the institution?

# Community Colleges

*Community needs.* What is happening in the local community? Because community colleges are local institutions serving primarily local needs, they have a special obligation to be responsive to changing community needs. What programs will serve it best in the next ten years? Is the problem one of consolidation and growth or of radical redirection?

*Expansion.* Should there be and can there be limits to further growth? Community colleges have been the fastest growing segment of postsecondary education. Should expansion be concentrated on one campus, or should multiple campuses be developed?

*Physical plant.* Is physical growth, even a change in location, going to be a major problem in the next few years? Because community colleges are a relatively recent development in American higher education, many have not had time or money to acquire adequate physical facilities for their rapidly increasing enrollments. Some people will relish the opportunity for growth; others will look upon it as a necessary evil. The choice of the new president will determine how well and enthusiastically it occurs.

*Financial crunch.* How important is someone with a sharp pencil and a keen eye for figures? The difficult times that affect all colleges and universities bear particularly heavily on community colleges. Periodic attempts at tax reform reflect citizen attitudes. The dependence of community colleges on local and state tax revenues makes them vulnerable. To what extent will the issue be one of holding the line or effecting reductions in budget?

*Community support.* Does the college have a problem in attracting community support? The goodwill of the local community is essential to the community college. Does the college image need refurbishing? Does it have the wholehearted support of community sponsors? How much attention will the new president need to give to this area?

*Politics.* Is the working relationship between the central state office and the local college satisfactory? As with state universities, community colleges must expect a high degree of public interest and often a considerable amount of public interference or attempted interference. Where community colleges are members of a statewide system, they face the same problems of autonomy that state universities face. Do state or county or local politics limit the college's freedom? How can political interference be kept to a minimum? If these are serious problems, it says something very important about the kind of man or woman who should be invited to cope with them.

# Exhibit C

# Sample Statements of Leadership Qualities

## Northeast Missouri State University

NMSU seeks a new president. This individual must possess high academic and personal standards, be energetic and persistent in the pursuit of excellence and be comfortable with the values and lifestyle of the University's region. The principal professional qualities sought are:

*Academic Leader* committed to high quality undergraduate liberal education and to its value in the disciplines of the liberal arts and sciences and in preprofessional education. Broadly familiar with assessment strategies appropriate to liberal education and in particular with the strengths and weaknesses of value-added assessment. Demonstrating in formal education and experience academic standards commensurate with the mission of NMSU and the goals of its faculty.

*Evaluator/Planner* committed to rigorous completion of the current five-year plan. Able to develop details for its implementation, while simultaneously advancing the aims of the plan into the next phase of development. Able to establish procedures for a continuous planning process. Able to balance a statewide liberal arts mission with local and regional service needs.

*Effective Administrator* possessing experience in administration at a high level in an institution at least equal in complexity and scope to NMSU. Able to discriminate between areas where further change should be encouraged and those which require increased stability. Willing to work with a campus administration that has purposefully been kept lean in comparison to investment in academic resources. Able to guide a gradual redistribution of resources to support services in a manner consistent with the maintenance of core educational goals. Sufficiently informed in key administrative areas, particularly budget and admissions. Able to balance administrative responsibilities with access for faculty, staff, and students. Able to select excellent staff. Able to delegate but be decisive.

*Community Developer* committed to the development of strong internal and external communities. Willing to value and encourage widespread understanding for and participation in major decisions affecting the University. Able to build bridges between external and internal communities. Particularly effective in interpreting the academic mission of the university, including the importance of assessment and its value in liberal education, to its various constituencies.

*Resource Acquirer* demonstrating by prior experience the personal and professional skills necessary to represent the University and it mission to the state of Missouri. Adept at creating and presenting the University's budgetary program. Knowledgeable about funding possibilities in the private sector.

## York College of Pennsylvania

York College of Pennsylvania offers quality, affordable undergraduate and graduate education which emphasizes both career education and the liberal arts. It offers 60 undergraduate programs and the M.B.A. degree. It has an enrollment of 2,600 full-time students and 1,500 part-time students in the evening and continuing education programs. The entering scores of students have progressed steadily in recent years. The College is debt-free and has a modern, well-maintained physical plant. Its endowment of $— million is equal to its annual operating budget, and the College has never suffered an annual operating deficit.

The next president of York College must possess integrity and high energy, preferably should have an earned doctorate, and in addition, demonstrate the following attributes:

### Academic

The president must understand the nature and purpose of undergraduate and graduate education. In particular, the individual must respect the qualities of good teaching and their application both to professional and liberal arts courses. He or she should be able to lead the College in a thorough review of its core curriculum. The president should assist the institution in establishing an effective balance between programs which generate enrollments and those necessary to maintain curricular integrity.

## Management

The president must demonstrate the ability to manage an enterprise at least equal in complexity to that of York College. He or she must be particularly skilled in fiscal management. On the whole, the board favors the continuation of the policy of fiscal conservatism that has served the College well for thirty-five years. At the same time, the new president will also be expected to use the College's current and expected future financial health to develop and encourage new educational ventures. Finally, the individual should be open to developing responsible participation of faculty and staff in the decision process.

## Planning

York College has gone through a decade of enrollment and physical growth. Some additional building will be necessary, but it must be carefully selected and be related to the fulfillment of specific program obligations in selected academic areas and student support services. The next president must understand planning and apply it in the creation of a comprehensive plan that recognizes existing commitments and identifies new opportunities. The president should be able to articulate a vision of the College's future and to involve the College community in its attainment.

## Community Relations

York College draws its students from all parts of the Mid-Atlantic region but it still retains a strong and special relation to the York County community. The president should be willing to be involved in that community. Such involvement should be an integral part of his or her past experience. The president should value the twelve thousand alumni of York College as a special element among its constituents and lead the College in even greater involvement of the alumni with its future.

## Human Relations

York College benefits from an informal, friendly campus atmosphere. Faculty are closely involved with students. The president must be comfortable with a high degree of personal interaction with the campus and all its constituent groups—faculty, students, and staff. The president should encourage high standards and high performance from all members of the campus community, creating incentives and encouragement which help produce those results.

*Resource Development*

The president should demonstrate knowledge of and, preferably, substantial prior experience with fund-raising and resource acquisition. For its future health, York College will rely on a combination of strong financial management of current operations, cultivation of local resources and the development of a larger base of donors, including alumni. The president will be expected to provide leadership and direction in this area and should consider it an area requiring a high degree of personal involvement.

# Exhibit D

## Sample Search Timetable

This sample calendar envisions a five-month or six-month search, beginning at the start of the academic year in September, taking into account the usual midwinter holiday, and concluding in March or April with the appointment of a president-elect who will take office in June or July. For an institution whose president has resigned a year in advance, this schedule is fairly typical; in other circumstances, the timetable may need to be adjusted.

**September**  Appoint search consultant. Draft statement of desired leadership qualities for circulation to campus constituencies. Draft and place advertising that incorporates desired leadership credentials and indicates November as the starting date for screening.

**October**  Advertising appears for four successive weeks. Board members, search committee members, others in academic community actively solicit nominations. Establish and staff search office; establish search committee procedures. Draft essential communications; assemble materials for mailing to applicants/ nominees.

**November**  Review applicant pool and reduce to top twenty candidates. Audit pool for appropriate range and diversity. Distill list of twenty candidates to eight-to-ten semifinalists; telephone to determine continuing interest and to request references.

**December**  Conduct reference checks. Plan off-campus interviews to take place after holidays; arrange housing, meals, and travel for candidates and search committee.

| | |
|---|---|
| **January** | Interview semifinalists off campus. Distill pool to three-to-five finalists. Telephone to determine continued interest and to advise of intensified background checks. |
| **January/February** | Plan two-day on-campus visit for each finalist and spouse; arrange travel and hospitality. Complete reference checks. |
| **February/March** | Complete finalists' visits to campus. Prepare and submit recommendations to the board. |
| **March/April** | Board negotiates terms; appoints and announces new president. |
| **April** | Appoint transition team. |
| **May/July** | Transition team prepares for arrival and successful first year. |

# Exhibit E

# Sample Search Budget

This search budget illustrates the range of probable costs for a presidential search. Costs will vary, of course, depending upon geographical location and salary scale. In general, the left column represents a minimum, while the right column approximates mid-range to high costs.

*Committee Staff:*
- Administrative Assistant (half-time) ................................... $12,000 – 20,000
- Clerk-Typist (part-time) .............................................. 6,000 – 10,000

*Office Expenses:*

Stationery ............................................................. 750 – 1,000
Telephone ............................................................. 1,000 – 1,500
Postage ............................................................... 750 – 1,200

*Advertising*

*Chronicle of Higher Education* ........................................ 3,500 – 3,500
Other journals (optional) ............................................. 5,000

*Candidate Travel:*

8–10 semifinalist interviews .......................................... 5,500 – 8,000
3 candidate/spouse campus visits ...................................... 4,400 – 6,000

*Search Committee Meetings*

Off-campus semifinalist interviews .................................... 4,200 – 6,850
6 committee meetings (hotel and travel) ............................... 9,600 – 14,400

***Consultant or Administrative Coordinator:*

Consultant (including travel) ......................................... 28,000– 55,000
OR
* Campus administrator
(one-third to one-half time release) .................................. 28,250– 50,000

**Total Costs:** ......................................................... $75,500– 132,450
OR

**$75,950– 127,450**

* Some institutions do not budget these items if time is "donated," but these are true costs.

**Note: Someone must direct the search. An experienced consultant can help to hold costs down. However, if a consultant is not engaged, a seasoned administrator (a dean or vice president) may assume that responsibility.

# Exhibit F

# Letter Soliciting Nominations

Date, 199_

Dr. Emily Stone
President
Valley Oak College
River City, TN 00000

PERSONAL AND CONFIDENTIAL

Dear President Stone:

I am writing to ask your assistance in nominating candidates for the position of president of Londonderry College, located in Augusta, Me. Following the resignation of President _____ , an interim president has been appointed to serve for the current academic year. The College is now seeking a new chief executive, one who will provide notable leadership at an important moment in the College's history. The anticipated date of appointment is July, 199_.

Londonderry College aspires to become Augusta's premier center for the education of women. Planning for the future is already under way; the next president of the College will have the opportunity to build a new kind of institution on a century-old foundation. I am writing to you in the hope that you may know of someone who would welcome this challenge and who has the ability to meet it.

I will appreciate your sending directly to me nominations of individuals you would consider suited for this appointment. To assist you, I have enclosed a statement of leadership qualities sought in the president as well as a brief institutional profile.

Sincerely yours,

Sharon Ross Perry
Trustee
Chair, Search Committee

# EXHIBIT G

# Letter of Thanks to Nominators

Date, 199__

Dr. William A. Jones
President
Valley Vista College
Vista, OR 00000

PERSONAL AND CONFIDENTIAL

Dear Dr. Jones:

Thank you for your nomination of _____ for the presidency of Londonderry College. The presidential search committee looks forward to learning more about this promising candidate.

I have already written to _____ to provide her with information about the College and to invite her interest in the presidency. The members of the search committee join me in hoping for an affirmative response.

Please accept from the trustees and the search committee our appreciation for your interest in Londonderry College and for your contribution to the successful outcome of the search for a new president.

Sincerely,

Trustee and Chair,
Presidential Search Committee

# Exhibit H

# Letter to Nominees Inviting Candidacy

Date, 199_

Dr. Taylor H. Cunningham
00 Winrock Road
Silver Spring, MD 20900

PERSONAL AND CONFIDENTIAL

Dear Dr. Cunningham:

It is a pleasure to inform you that you have been nominated for the presidency of Londonderry College. The search committee hopes that you will agree to be considered for this vital post.

To assist you in deciding if you wish to become a candidate, I am enclosing a fact sheet describing Londonderry College as well as a statement of the leadership qualities sought by the board of trustees in the next president. Should you decide to pursue this opportunity, I will appreciate receiving a current resume and a letter of interest.

Please be assured that all nominations will be treated in confidence. The search committee will begin reviewing credentials during the last week in February with appointment of the new president anticipated in late spring.

The search committee will welcome an affirmative decision. I look forward to your reply with great interest.

Sincerely,


Trustee and Chair,
Presidential Search Committee

# Exhibit I

## Equal Opportunity Recruitment Sources

*Publications:*

*Black Issues in Higher Education*
10520 Warwick Ave., Suite B-8
Fairfax, Va. 22030

*Affirmative Action Register*
8356 Olive Blvd.
St. Louis, Mo. 63132

The following organizations are prepared to make recommendations of qualified women and minority-group members for consideration by search and selection committees. Committees are urged to consult them and to solicit their aid in identifying prospective candidates.

***For women:***

Office of Women in Higher Education
American Council on Education
*Suite 887, One Dupont Circle*
*Washington, D.C. 20036*

American Association of Women in
Community and Junior Colleges
*Suite 410, One Dupont Circle*
*Washington, D.C. 20036*

National Association for Women Deans,
Administrators and Counselors
*Suite 624A, 1625 Eye Street, N.W.*
*Washington, D.C. 20006*

*For minorities:*

Office of Minority Concerns
American Council on Education
*Suite 800, One Dupont Circle*
*Washington, D.C. 20036*

National Association for Equal Opportunity
in Higher Education
*2243 Wisconsin Avenue, N.W.*
*Washington, D.C. 20007*

National Community College Hispanic Council
American Association of Community
and Junior Colleges
*Suite 410, One Dupont Circle*
*Washington, D.C. 20036*

National Council on Black American Affairs
American Association of Community
and Junior Colleges
*Suite 410, One Dupont Circle*
*Washington, D.C. 20036*

# EXHIBIT J

# Letter Acknowledging Application

(mark personal, send to home address, if possible)

Date, 199_

Dear _____:

Thank you for your statement of interest in Londonderry College and your application for the position of president. The search committee will begin reviewing all applications and nominations approximately (date), and within a short time thereafter will provide you with a statement on the status of your candidacy.

The College and the search committee extend their thanks to you for your willingness to be considered for the presidency of Londonderry College.

Sincerely,

Trustee and Chair,
Search Committee

# Exhibit K

# Letter Terminating Candidacy

March 18, 1991

Dr. Maureen L. Evans
65 Old County Road
Hampden, ME 04444

PERSONAL AND CONFIDENTIAL

Dear Dr. Evans:

The Presidential Search Committee for Londonderry College met recently to review the credentials of applicants and nominees. Londonderry College was especially fortunate to attract a substantial pool of highly accomplished candidates. The Committee's primary task, therefore, was to select from among this distinguished group those who appeared best suited to our College's very particular needs at this point in our history.

In this spirit we studied your application with great care and were favorably impressed by your many attainments. We recognized that you could bring to Londonderry College much that would be of value. Nonetheless, the Committee finally judged that your background and experience do not correspond fully to the College's needs at the present time, and we have thus terminated your candidacy.

The Search Committee asked me to convey, on their behalf and that of the Trustees, our warm appreciation for your interest in Londonderry College.

Sincerely,

Trustee and Chair,
Presidential Search Committee

# Exhibit L

## Questions on Candidates' Minds

Below is a sampling of the kinds of questions candidates are likely to ask. When designing the schedules for campus visits, the committee should make sure that each candidate will have the opportunity to talk with people who know the answers and are prepared to state them frankly.

### On finances

Has the institution generated operating surpluses or operating deficits in the last five years?

How much indebtedness exists? Of what nature?

Has the institution recently experienced any cash-flow difficulties?

What is the condition of the physical plant? Have laboratories been updated? Is the library automated? What additional facilities are needed?

Have there been any developments that would significantly affect the nature of the institution's traditional sources of revenue or the level of support?

For private institutions: What is the overall strategy for raising revenue from private sources? When was the last capital campaign? What was the goal and outcome? Is there need for a major fund-raising campaign? How has support from private sources changed over the last few years?

For public institutions: What has been the recent record of the legislature regarding appropriations to the institution? How do the institution's appropriations, state and federal, compare with appropriations for other institutions in the state? Has there been any attempt to raise funds from private sources?

For community colleges: What are the primary funding sources? Can local support, in taxes or donations, be counted on? What are the local problems, if any?

### On faculty

Which are the strongest (and the weakest) departments, schools, areas of instruction or research?

What is the rate of faculty turnover? Is there a tenure problem?

Is faculty morale good, bad, or neutral?

Is there an affirmative-action plan?

Is there a faculty union? Interest in one? What is the institution's position on unionization?

Have recent accreditation reviews resulted in any recommendations for significant changes? If so, what changes were recommended, and how have they been dealt with?

### On administration

What does the table of organization look like?

Where is the administration strongest, where the weakest? Are there serious problems in the administrative area?

### On students

Has the student body changed in size or composition over the last five years? What is anticipated over the next five?

Is there a dropout problem? How serious?

What percentage of the students are receiving financial aid?

What is the recruitment program? Is there an effort to attract and retain minorities? Nontraditional students?

### On the board of trustees

How strong, interested, and active is the board?

What does the board see as its role in governance?

Is there mutual trust among board, faculty, and administration?

If a multicampus system, how much autonomy has each campus?

How much authority resides in the central system office and how much in state offices or with officials such as the budget officer, the commissioner of education, the governor?

### On public relations

Is there a town-gown problem? If so, what has caused it and what can be done about it?

How is the institution regarded by the press?

Does the institution have the wholehearted support of its alumni?

For public institutions: What liaison exists between the institution and the state department of education, the governor's office, the legislature?

For church-related institutions: Is the college or university controlled by, supported by, or independent of the parent religious denomination?

### In general

What are the major strengths of the institution? Its major weaknesses?

What are the most serious problems needing attention?

What are the three most important contributions a new president could make?

### On terms of appointment

What can I expect as compensation?

What are the fringe benefits?

Does the college or university provide housing?

# Exhibit M

# Examples of Materials Provided to Candidates

*To Applicants and Nominees:*
The catalogue.
The student "view book."
The statement of leadership qualities.
A summary of institutional characteristics.

*To Semifinalists:*
The president's report for the last three years.
The executive summary from the latest accreditation report.
Specialized program brochures.
Institutional research studies.
Long-term planning documents.
The faculty and staff handbook.

*To Finalists:*
The current budget in its entirety.
Detailed information on capital campaigns.
Minutes of major board meetings.

# Exhibit N

## Sample Schedule For Campus Visit

### Day One

8:00    Breakfast with President's Cabinet or Trustees Executive Committee or Search Committee Chair

9:00    One-hour meetings with chief academic officer, chief student affairs officer, chief financial officer, chief institutional advancement officer

1:00    Lunch and meeting with academic division heads

3:00    Meeting with faculty senate or faculty representatives

4:30    Meeting with alumni

5:30    Relaxation time

6:30    Dinner and meeting with student leaders
(Spouse might be included)

### Day Two

8:00    Breakfast with community representatives

9:30    Coffee hour (open invitation to entire campus community)

11:00   Campus tour (or optional meetings)

12:00   Lunch with Trustees Executive Committee

1:00    Meeting with Trustees Executive Committee

*Note:  Spouse will need independently planned schedule for Day One, but might be included in student dinner and in morning activities on Day Two. Spouse might welcome relaxation time or independent exploration while candidate is meeting with trustees.*

# Exhibit O

# Announcement of Selection

FOR IMMEDIATE RELEASE

MARCH 15, 19__

In concluding a national search, the Board of Trustees of Midwestern College are pleased to announce the appointment of Barbara Jones as tenth president of the College. Dr. Jones will succeed James Whitley who retires on July 1, after fifteen years as President. Dr. Jones will assume the presidency on that date.

Barbara Jones was chosen by the Board with the strong recommendation of a twelve-person search committee and after equally positive reactions from the college community. In choosing Dr. Jones, the Board and the Search Committee found her to be the right new leader for Midwestern College after considering the qualifications of more than one hundred candidates for the presidency.

Dr. Jones received her B.A. in history from Duke University and her Ph.D. in the same field from Washington University of Saint Louis. She has published extensively in the contemporary history of Mexico and has held faculty appointments at Hood College and the University of Massachusetts. Dr. Jones comes to Midwestern College from the position of provost at the State University of New York at Binghamton.

In welcoming Barbara Jones to Midwestern College, Chair of the Board of Trustees Thomas Smith also praised the search committee and its chair, Trustee William Benjamin, for a job well done in conducting the search on behalf of the college.

# RESOURCES

Estela Mara Bensimon, Marian L. Gade, and Joseph F. Kauffman, *On Assuming a College or University Presidency*, American Association for Higher Education, 1989.

*CEO, 1991 Compensation, Benefits, and Conditions of Employment for College and University Chief Executives*, College & University Personnel Association, 1991. (Published every two years.)

*Deciding Who Shall Lead*, American Council on Education and Association of Governing Boards of Universities and Colleges, 1986.

Madeline F. Green, *The American College President*, American Council on Education, 1988.

Theodore J. Marchese and Jane Fiori Lawrence, *The Search Committee Handbook*, American Association for Higher Education, 1989.

Judith B. McLaughlin and David Riesman, *Choosing a College President*, The Carnegie Foundation for the Advancement of Teaching, 1990.

Charles B. Neff, *Search Tips*, Association of Governing Boards of Universities and Colleges, 1991.

Charles B. Neff, "The Transitional Presidency," *AGB Reports*, September/October 1989.

Roberta H. Ostar, *Public Roles, Private Lives*, Association of Governing Boards of Universities and Colleges, 1991.

Dale Parnell and Margaret Rivera, *Contracts, Salaries, and Compensation*, American Association of Community and Junior Colleges, 1991.

Robert H. Wellen and Howard L. Clemons, *Presidential Housing and Tax Reform*, American Association of State Colleges and Universities and National Association of Colleges and University Attorneys, 1987.